Architectural Guide
Hong Kong

D1478784

Architectural Guide
Hong Kong

Ulf Meyer

DOM
publishers

Hong Kong Island (Central/Western) 28

Hong Kong Island (Wan Chai/Eastern/Southern) 84

One Peking

The Masterpiece

Peninsula Hotel

Cultural Centre

Two IFC

Bank of China

Cheung Kong Centre

CITIC Tower

HKCEC

Yau Tong

North Point

Causeway Bay

Cross-Harbour Tunnel

The Peak

Pacific Place

Bank of China

One IFC

Two IFC

Central Plaza

Cultural Centre

Old Station Tower

Two IFC

Jardine House

Bank of China

One Peking

Harbour City

The Center

Shun Tak Centre

Hong Kong Macau
Ferry Terminal
China and Macau

Kowloon Park

Ocean Terminal

Ocean Centre

Lantau Island

Western Tunnel

One Peking

The Harbourside

ICC Tower

Clearwater Bay, Saikung

Marina Cove Properties, Saikung

Townhouses above Sheung Wan beach, Saikung

The Sky above Hong Kong

Hong Kong, Chinese for "fragrant harbour", was the first city in East Asia that I ever visited. I will never forget the cultural shock I felt when I stepped outside the airport terminal at Kai Tak in 1995. This was the beginning of my enthusiasm for the cities of East Asia, which in the meantime made me come back to this part of the world dozens of times. Hong Kong is one of the most un-exotic cities in East Asia, especially when it was "British" still.

Nevertheless, Hong Kong's visitors are immediately taken: The city's location on the water, the high mountains and the narrow urban strip in between, its forced drive into the sky, have led to the development of the most breathtaking skyline in the world. Since my first trip Hong Kong has continued to grow into the sky, while the harbour (through the ubiquitous land reclamation) is getting smaller and smaller all the time. Today Kai Tak is history and Hong Kong is no longer British—but it is not quite Chinese just yet either. But the Chinese sister cities around Hong Kong have awakened in the meantime: Guangzhou is now the capital of the most productive industrial region of the world, Macau is the largest gambling city in the world (beating Las Vegas), Shenzhen an economically highly successful B-version of Hong Kong. Even Zhuhai has pulled itself out of the swamps of the Pearl River Delta and blossomed to become a sub-centre of the region. In particular the eastern shore of the Pearl River today is the most important axis in the new urban network of South China. Despite the new competition, Hong Kong is still unique—in its ambition, elegance, ruthlessness, density and cosmopolitan aura. It does not need to fear the new competition from its sisters across the border. As a "Special Administrative Region" of China Hong Kong is still getting special treatment—for its own benefit, even if today the main- and motherland sends not only cars with right-hand steering wheel, but also pregnant women by the tens of thousands, who ask for admittance at the border. SARS and the Asian economic crisis have meanwhile come over the city, but did not harm it in the long term. Its role as a financial centre of the (Asian) world has been strengthened and its proximity to the world's manufacturing centre in Guangdong is still its trump card. The only threat Hong Kong faces is to be the victim of its own success. Air pollution has increased significantly and even the most beautiful skyline in the world will not impress visitors when it remains hidden behind a grey-wet wall of particles.

The architecture of the city, to be dealt with in this book, has not changed in principle between my first and my last visit, only radicalised. And that is despite the fact that it was already quite radical before. Hong Kong is home to more skyscrapers than any other city in the world. It is hardly an exaggeration to say that nearly every building here is a skyscraper. There are more than

Sensual compactness: skyscrapers in Wan Chai

The Peak

Between Happy Valley and Kowloon

2,300 buildings with a height of over 100 metres. This number is growing daily. The narrow towers look like high-powered, thin asparagus. The journey on the Star Ferry between Hong Kong Island and its commercial centre and Central Kowloon Peninsula is like a trip through a clearing in the forest of high-rises.

The "unintentional beauty" that produces the artificial stalagmite maze of towers is "a creature of chance," as Siegfried Kracauer called it. No one has ever planned it, it just happened and tomorrow will no longer be the same. Today Kowloon, traditionally the "bad side" of Hong Kong, is also a rocketing high-rise city. That was not the case on my first visit, because then, the Jumbo jets still flew low and with a deafening roar above the rooftops of Kowloon.

When in the city, it is hard to believe what the statistics say about Hong Kong: that of the 1,100 square kilometres that make up the territory, only 25% are built up. But a bus ride to Victoria Island, for example, or to the New Territories makes it clear to everyone immediately that it is steep slopes the up to 550 metres tall, and the 262 small and micro-islands, that belong to the metropolitan area. The urbanisation machine for the time being had to stop in the face of the rugged topography that makes up the bulk of the urban area. The need for expansion space

Ultra-compact residential buildings in Man Sing Street in Jordan

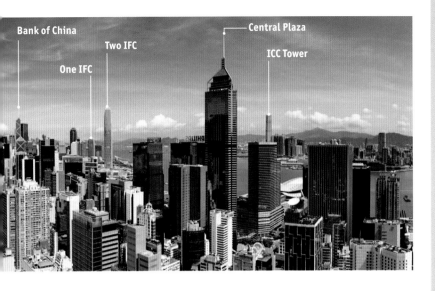

Bank of China
Two IFC
One IFC
Central Plaza
ICC Tower

in all three dimensions continues and so the topography of the island is becoming ever more man-made: mountains are capped and their dirt used for landfills and land reclamation projects: thus creating two new (construction) sites simultaneously. The original wild, now largely domesticated topography of the island seems to be exhausted. Its limits are absolute and almost all possible landfill spots have already been taken from the sea: almost all of Victoria Island is made up of steep slopes, which are not easily built upon. At the same time, the difficult terrain is a huge benefit for the city, for only because of that did the perpetual urbanisation steamroller make

a bow around the hills and did the city therefore maintain a beautiful green carpet of vegetation as its background.

At least as long as the largely democratic political and liberal economic system of Hong Kong remains (50 years, that is) and the area's own currency retains its validity, as long as Deng Xiaoping's doctrine of "one country, two systems" stays true, Hong Kong will not feel like "the third-largest metropolis in China" but stay deliberately different from Beijing and Shanghai. Already, Hong Kong is one of the cities with the highest cost of living in the world, but that does not diminish its appeal. On the contrary, high living costs often translate into high wages

Here, as on many other Asian construction sites, bamboo scaffolding is part of everyday life.

Asia Life Building

The banks of Victoria Harbour with the Asia Life Building in the foreground (around 1900)

for unskilled labour. Workers and house-maids from the Philippines and Indonesia especially appreciate this and migrate to the city in large numbers. But the largest group of immigrants is the Chinese themselves: In 1949, at the end of the Chinese Civil War, the first great wave of migration from China spilled over into Hong Kong. To build a roof over the heads of the mostly poor newcomers, Hong Kong began a massive housing programme, which still shapes the city significantly today. Small and very simple apartments in high-rise buildings for almost two million people were built out of the blue. Whole vast new neighbourhoods emerged from the drawing boards of the planners of the city council and housing associations. Residential living in the hyper-capitalist city is predominantly proto-"socialist." Only since the 1980s, when incomes had stabilised for a broad section of society at an acceptable level, have the simplest of housing estates been replaced with more comfortable ones or at least been reno-vated. At the same time many were con-verted to rental apartments.

Hong Kong, with a population density of more than 6,000 inhabitants per square kilometre, is one of the most densely populated areas in the world: its popu-lation has increased twelve-fold since 1945 (from 600,000 to 7,000,000). The city is highly compressed, one might even say "overpopulated". Almost all of the population lives in high-rise build-ings, because Hong Kong is a city with almost no individual family homes. It is the vertical city *par excellence*. Because of its rapid de-industrialisation, the city

found its salvation in trade and finance and has done so with great success. Hong Kong can look back onto a strong eco-nomic tradition. Trading was once the *raison d'etre* of the city, even when the first Portuguese traders landed on the coast of Hong Kong. More than a century later, the British East India Company came to China for the first time and their flourishing trade in opium led not only to the first Opium War, but subsequent-ly to the occupation of Hong Kong by the British in 1841. Thus Hong Kong is based on being "a borrowed place with limited time". After the status of the city was consolidated as an official British colony in 1843, the British also wanted Kowloon and later the area north of Kowloon up to the Shenzhen River from China to ex-pand the territory. Hong Kong has since been an island (Victoria) and a peninsula (Kowloon). The newly acquired hinter-land was as important for the supply of fresh water and food in Hong Kong as it still is today, because the city can not sustain itself. It survives on trade. This did not change when during World War II, the Japanese overtook Hong Kong and the city was under the rule of Tenno in Tokyo.

Hong Kong has been booming for the last 170 years. Since the 1930s, Hong Kong has been a city of a million people. In the late 1940s it already had two million in-habitants. Until the crucial date in Chi-nese 20th-century history, 1949, Hong Kong was economically and politically in the shadow of Shanghai. But with the ad-vent of communist rule in the vast empire of China, Hong Kong started to use its

Victoria Peak

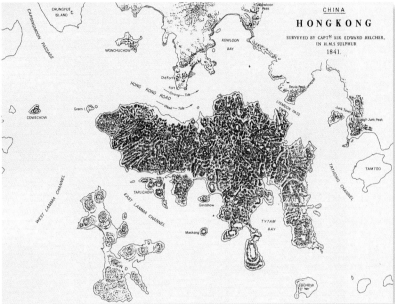

Map of Hong Kong Island, charted by Sir Edward Belcher (1841)

beneficial role as a free-trade zone and outmanoeuvered its rival Shanghai. From the newly established People's Republic of China not only hundreds of thousands of migrants fled to Hong Kong, but also many companies moved their headquarters to Hong Kong. Shanghai's weakness became Hong Kong's strength. In 1935 the new headquarters of the HSBC bank was built and with it a new era had dawned in Hong Kong architecture: the Bank was fully air-conditioned and even had a modern elevator — it became the prototype of the new Hong Kong.

A devastating fire in a slum in 1953 had caused a hasty emergency construction programme for the newly homeless. In the following year the central "Hong Kong Housing Authority" was established and eventually turned around the entire city, filling it with its giant subsidised residential complexes. Until the mid-1950s Hong Kong was made up of mostly four- to five-storey buildings. But that was soon over: the city grew rapidly in the third dimension and has since become the largest high-rise city in the world.

Since the 1970s nine new towns have been established around the city, and the corresponding construction programme was the largest in the world. Almost 2.5 million people live in these new towns today, which are created as separate towns, with their own jobs and social and transport infrastructure. There is no room for private gardens or cars in them, but the transport connections are good: every single day, more than nine million

Billboards in Kowloon

passengers use the public transport system in Hong Kong, one of the most modern in the world.

Hong Kong's meteoric rise to become the centre of East Asia was challenged only after Deng Xiaoping's economic opening of China. The nearby village of Shenzhen was turned into a "Special Economic Zone", which quickly became a thriving metropolis on the doorstep of Hong Kong. But Shenzhen never will outdo Hong Kong. On the contrary, today the two cities are complementary.

When in the 1980s Britain had to start organising its withdrawal from Hong Kong, many residents turned their back on the city. Beijing's Tiananmen Square massacre of 1989 made the city's future as a "Special Administrative Region" of China look less rosy. Because Britain was not willing to allow Hong Kong residents to immigrate to the United Kingdom, a "second, Canadian Hong Kong" was set up in Vancouver (BC), which flourishes to this day.

With the demolition of the famous "Walled City" in 1992 and the relocation of the airport (and with it its noise and danger), Kowloon has been significantly upgraded. The former airport is now a building site. Meanwhile, the renovation of the early makeshift settlements

is a major urban issue, because the poor quality of the hastily raised tower blocks has become quite obvious and visible in places.

When on July 1st 1997, the People's Republic of China took control of Hong Kong, the world held its breath for a moment. Opinions differ about whether the city has since changed to its advantage or disadvantage. Democratic rights and journalistic freedom must be defended daily in Hong Kong today. In terms of tourism and the economy, however, there is no doubt that Hong Kong's role as an export machine and engine of growth across the region remains true. The appeal of the city for Chinese youth from the "mainland" seeking work is unbroken: Hong Kong not only promises good wages and better medical care than many places in China, but also the city does not follow the infamous "one-child policy". Babies born in Hong Kong enjoy automatic right of citizenship. However, not only poor migrant workers or pregnant women feel magnetised by Hong Kong, affluent home buyers are also flocking to the city: every third property goes to a buyer from the mainland, and these numbers are rising. Hong Kong's retail industry has also discovered the high-spending mainlanders and adjusted its range

to suit the taste (or lack thereof) of the Nouveau Riche from China. Hong Kong is a shopping paradise and popular harbinger of the western world: with its own Disneyland, 800 kilometres of coastline, 235 islands and a mega-airport whose connections reach into every corner of the world, Hong Kong is the gateway to southern China and the Pearl River Delta region. Ferries and increasingly bridges connect Hong Kong with Macao, Zhuhai, Guangzhou and the countless coastal towns of southern China, which today represent an economic unit. Tens of millions of Chinese in the Pearl River Delta work for outsourced Hong Kong companies. Hong Kong is no longer an ex-colonial island, but the centre of a mega-city in the Delta, which has more than 40 million inhabitants.

Hong Kong has a reputation of being a commercial stronghold, but a cultural desert. In fact, Hong Kong has maintained more traditional Chinese culture than some places in China, because the city has been spared the Cultural Revolution and served as a refuge for artists from China. Wong Kar-Wai, whose internationally acclaimed films gave the city a cinematic reputation, is just one example of successful global cultural production "made in Hong Kong". In terms of architectural and urban design, however, the city constantly eats itself: the ongoing economic and housing boom in one of the most liberal market economies of the world killed almost all European-style pre-war buildings. Only very occasionally a British colonial building still peeks between the skyscrapers. The remaining colonial buildings can now be counted on one or two hands.

Architecturally, four major offices in Hong Kong ride the tiger: Wong & Ouyang, Dennis Lau, Rocco Yim and P & T have shaped the city with their buildings persistently. In the city, they compete with each other as well as with the development of the Chinese market. At the same time, Hong Kong has proven to be fertile ground for foreign architects: European and American architects in particular have contributed to the city and its breathtaking skyline, unrivalled in the world. Famous western architects such as Pei, Rudolph, Foster and Seidler have shaped the skyline of Victoria with their towers. But the foreign influence on Hong Kong's architecture is not always as visible: Nearly half of the approximately one thousand architects in Hong Kong are either foreigners or have studied abroad and bring ideas from different parts of the world back to Hong Kong.

1 Hong Kong Island: Central/Western

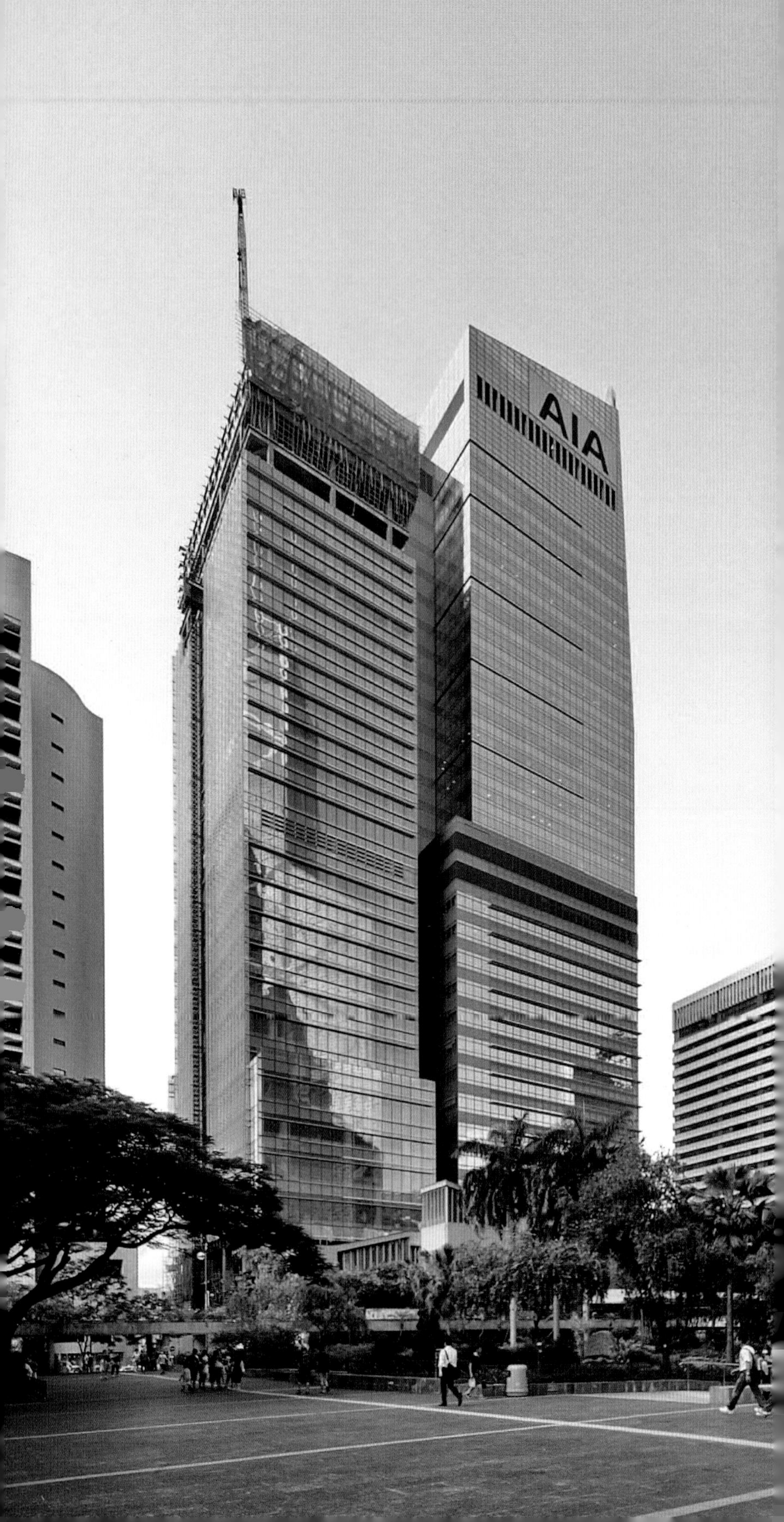
AIA

AIG Tower «

1 Connaught Road, Central
Skidmore, Owings and Merrill
2005

001 B

This 185-metre-high skyscraper for the American International Group (AIG) was designed by Skidmore, Owings and Merrill (SOM) of Chicago. For decades, this practice has planned most of the world's high-rises. The plot of the new 40-storey office tower was formerly occupied by the Furama Kempinski Hotel. It was demolished in 2001. The AIG Corp. is a major user of the building, which is shaped to look like a traditional Chinese junk. The client merged two plots of land for its construction and sold shares in the hotel property to the Pidemco Corp. and AIG. Pidemco is part of the Temasek Group of Singapore. In 2009 the name of the building was modified from AIG Tower into AIA Central because the AIG Corp. was at the heart of the financial crisis in 2009.

Bank of America Tower ≽

12 Harcourt Road, Admiralty
Ho & Partners Architects
1975

002 D

The skyscraper for the Bank of America is special in the context of the skyline of Hong Kong: not because of its architectural design, but because it is one of the few skyscrapers in the city with a perforated façade. The 38-storey tower with a height of 146 metres has horizontal, rectangular punched windows in a white façade. The building is also known as Gammon House.

Bank of China Tower

1 Garden Road
I. M. Pei
1990

003 B

1

The prismatic tower of the Bank of China is one of the tallest skyscrapers in Hong Kong, with great recognition value. It is the headquarters of the influential Chinese state-owned bank in Hong Kong. The tower is 307 metres tall; the two antennas on the roof even reach 360 metres into the sky. The Bank of China Tower was the tallest in the city and throughout Asia from 1989 to 1992 and the first building outside the USA to be more than 1,000 feet tall. Today it is only the fourth-tallest tower in the city. It stands on 6,700 square metres of land that was formerly the site of the Murray House, which has been relocated to Stanley. The Hong Kong government sold the property in 1982 for HK $ 1 billion. This was seen as a relatively cheap price and thus a preference for Chinese buyers, as previously the local subway company MTR had paid almost double that amount for a similar-sized property in the Admiralty. When this became known, there was a momentary loss of confidence in the Hong Kong Stock Exchange and the stock index and the exchange rate of the Hong Kong dollar fell the following day. The plans of the Chinese state-owned bank were seen as a symbol of the new rulers after the surrender of the British crown colony to Beijing. Originally, the tower was to be inaugurated on August 8th of 1988, because the number 8 is considered to be a lucky number in China. However, there were some construction delays and the deadline could not be met. The Bank of China in Hong Kong (BOCHK) itself uses only the top four and the lower 19 floors of the building; the other floors are rented out. A small observation deck on the 43rd floor is publicly accessible. The 72-storey building has access to the underground station "Central" and is the first high-rise building with a "composite space frame". On a square base of 52 x 52 metres the building is divided diagonally into four triangles. Each quarter of the floor plan reaches up to a different height in the sky, while the southern block reaches to the full height. The diagonals are marked in the façade with white bands. The skyscraper has no "front" side, but acts as a dynamic sculpture from all sides. Inside, there are no structural supports; diagonal loads are routed to the four large corner columns. The expressive form of the structure was compared to bamboo. The tower has a blue glass curtain wall. The design was controversial because the Bank of China had not consulted a feng shui master before construction, as is common practice in Hong Kong. In this regard, the sharp corners and X-forms of the building's façade were considered to be an unfortunate choice. The plot is very steep with the main entrance on the south and the side entrance several floors up in the north. A large lobby hall with escalators links both sides, while the main hall has a trim of green marble. To the north there is a 15-storey tall atrium, and the base is clad in granite.

Flagstaff House

10 Cotton Tree Drive, Central
Murdoch Bruce
1846

Flagstaff House in Hong Kong Park is the oldest British colonial building in Hong Kong. Until 1932 it was the commander of the British Army's residence and now is a museum of tea culture and a popular backdrop for wedding photography. The property is situated at a steep slope above the Queen's Road barracks, which once was the embankment before land-fills pushed the coastline out further. Flagstaff House was designed in a neo-classical style by Murdoch Bruce and Lieutenant Bernard. The west and east wings were destroyed by the Japanese army during the Second World War. After the takeover of Hong Kong by the Japanese, Flagstaff House was repaired and served as the residence of the Japanese commander. After World War II it was used by the British commander again — until 1978, when he moved into a new building on Barker Road. Thereafter Flagstaff House was handed over to the Government of Hong Kong and in 1989 was declared a monument. It was renovated extensively and its structure was strengthened. In 1984 the "Museum of Tea Ware" was opened, and a new wing was added in 1995.

Lippo Centre

89 Queensway, Admiralty
Paul Rudolph, Wong & Ouyang
1988

The Lippo Centre is a double tower, whose unusual blue curtain wall façades evoke koala bears climbing a tree. There are three large bay windows on top of one another, rotating around the structure. The supporting columns are visible only at the base of the tower. The design results in a total of 58 different office floor plans. Both towers have hexagonal floor plans with 36 and 40 floors and stand on a common, four-storey podium. Today the building is owned and used by Indonesia's Lippo Bank. At the time of construction the building was, however, known as "Bond Centre". The towers are 186 metres tall and vertically divided into three parts. They were designed by American

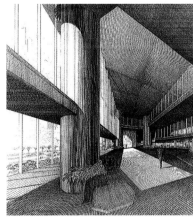

architect Paul Rudolph, who was very active in East Asia. The glass façades were imported from the USA. The skyscrapers are accessed both at street level and on the elevated skywalk level. The large foyer is planted and covered with pink-coloured Spanish granite.

Standard Chartered Bank

2 Queen's Road, Central

P & T

1990

006 B

The British Standard Chartered Bank plays a prominent role in the financial world of Hong Kong because it is one of the banks that issue currency (banknotes) in the city-state since there is no central bank in Hong Kong. In 1859 the "Chartered Bank of India, Australia and China" was founded and opened its first branch in Hong Kong. Just three years later it began to circulate the Hong Kong dollar. The current headquarters building of the bank is a narrow tower, next to the (previously also British) Hong Kong & Shanghai Bank. Designed by P & T Architects, its stone-perforated façade is a typical example of the high-rise architecture of the late

1980s. The 185-metre-tall skyscraper with 42 floors is owned by the Hang Lung Group. A previous building on the site was only 79 metres tall and was also designed by P & T, completed in 1959. In the 1980s the Bank's home became too small. It holds a license agreement for the property to the year 2854. The Hang Lung Group leased a large part of the 22,000 square metres of floor space to the bank. The headquarters of the Bank is now located in another building in Millennium City 1. Like a cascade, the façades jump back from the 17th floor to the top of the tower, receding every six floors in several steps. The corners are cut at 45-degree angles to improve visibility and light conditions. The façades are clad in pink and beige granite, while a grand stair leads up to the main entrance on the first floor.

HSBC Main Building

1 Queen's Road Central, Central
Norman Foster
1985

007 B

The main building of the Hong Kong and Shanghai Banking Corporation (HSBC) is one of the best known high-rise buildings in Hong Kong. It is a good example of the British hi-tech architecture of the 1980s. The building is located prominently on the southern edge of Statue Square. With a height of 178 metres and 44 floors, it is not one of the tallest skyscrapers in the city, but during its construction it was the most expensive building ever to be built. For its construction, the previous bank building dating from 1935 was pulled down. The new high-rise building consists of steel frames, which were prefabricated in the UK. The elevators stop only at select floors, from which there is access to the desired floors via escalators. The offices are column-free. Large computer-controlled mirrors follow the sun, bringing daylight into the atrium. Sun shades in front of the façades reduce heat levels in summer, and sea water is used to cool the building. The offices have raised floors, under which power and data cables and outlets are installed. All parts were prefabricated in different countries: the glass, and aluminium panels came from the U. S. and the space cells from Japan, for example. The façades are shaped by their structure that resembles a shelf. They are suspended from large, double-storey beams in stacks that become smaller the higher up on the building they are. There are eight groups of four steel columns clad in aluminium. From there on five levels, the diagonal tension members are suspended. This method arose from the original idea of the skyscraper being built over the old building, which would have remained in operation until completion of the new building above. Today 5,000 people work in the building. The HSBC Main Building is one of the earliest masterpieces of architect Lord Norman Foster of London, who was able to design all construction details, including the furniture. In plan, the tower is a simple rectangle divided along its long side into three wide and four narrow strips. There is no large foyer, but a public space under the building. From there, diagonally placed escalators bring people up through a glass floor into the 14-storey banking hall. The offices are open with galleries towards the atrium. The HSBC Main Building has a hill behind to the South and a clear view of the sea to the North: an ideal situation, according to Feng Shui. On weekends and public holidays, the space underneath the building acts as a meeting place for the cleaning ladies and nannies from the Philippines who work in Hong Kong. In 2006 a lobby on the ground floor was added, designed by "One Space".

Legislative Council Building ≈ `008` B

8 Jackson Road, Central
Sir Aston Webb and Ingress Bell
1912

From 1985 to 2011 this building was used as the seat of the Legislative Council, the Parliament of Hong Kong. The architects of the building, Webb and Bell, had previously designed the east front of Buckingham Palace in London. The granite-clad building in Hong Kong with Ionic columns has circumferential arcades on two levels. The central granite dome carries a lantern with a Tudor crown. Only the two hipped roofs on the left and right of the dome are built in a Chinese style, with a wooden substructure and clad in black tiles. During Japanese rule over Hong Kong, the building was used as the headquarters of the Japanese military police. Since the Parliament moved to Tamar, the building has been used as a courthouse.

Prince's Building ≽ `009` B

10 Chater Road, Central
P & T
1965

The Prince's Building is an office and retail building with 29 floors. The name was taken from the previous building on the same site, a four-storey building dating from 1904 in the Neo-Renaissance style. It was demolished in 1963. The new building with a plain white façade grid is, like most buildings in the quarter, owned by the Hong Kong Land Corp. It frames Statue Square from the west.

Mandarin Oriental Hotel
5 Connaught Road, Central
Leigh & Orange
1963

010 B

The Mandarin Oriental Hotel was built in 1963 after a design by Leigh & Orange. At 26 floors it offers 501 guest rooms, ten restaurants and a three-storey spa with pool, gym and hairdresser. The famous Queen's Building once stood on the site. The interior design is by Don Ashton, an art director from Hollywood. The Mandarin Oriental Hotel has long been the tallest building in Hong Kong. It was the first hotel in the city to offer its guests direct-dial telephones in every room and the first in Asia where each room had its own bathroom. The ballroom is large enough for 600 guests. The hotel was extensively renovated in 2005, however the lobby and bars were retained.

Jardine House

1 Connaught Place, Central
P&T
1973

When Jardine House was inaugurated in 1973, it was the tallest skyscraper in Hong Kong and Asia at 178 metres and 52 floors (until 1980 when it was surpassed by the Hopewell Centre). Jardine House is owned — like many of the neighbouring buildings — by the Hong Kong Land Corp. which has connected their buildings to each other with pedestrian bridges. The new building replaced the 16-storey Jardine House, built in 1948, which was sold as the company combined sites for the construction of the Landmark and the Wheelock Towers nearby. Jardine House stands on reclaimed land and enjoys the written privilege that no building shall be constructed to its north side, which would harm views of the harbour. The neighbouring site, on which the main post office was built, is only permitted to build up to a maximum height of 37 metres. The steel skeleton of the Jardine building is filled in with a curtain wall featuring round porthole windows. Between the inner core and the façade there are no columns. The Jardine Corp. is a multi-national conglomerate active in the real estate, hotel, construction, retail, finance and car industries. It was founded in Guangzhou in 1832 and originally traded tea, silk and opium.

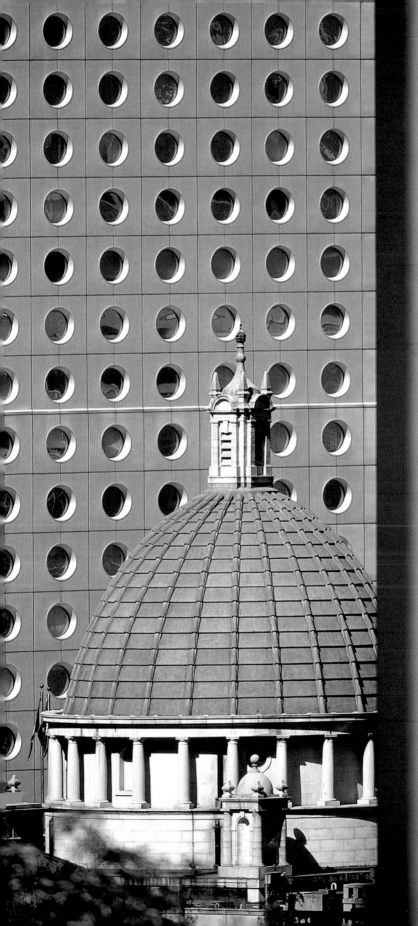

One IFC

012 B

8 Finance Street, Central
César Pelli with Rocco Design
1999

One International Finance Centre belongs to a new building complex on the Central waterfront, which also includes a second high rise, a shopping mall and the 55-storey Four Seasons Hotel. It is 210 metres tall and has 39 floors. 5,000 people work in the building, and it has a mall at the base containing 200 shops.

Two IFC

013 B

8 Finance Street, Central
César Pelli with Rocco Design
2003

At a height of 415 metres, the Two IFC tower is currently the second-tallest building in the city. It has 88 office floors and 22 trading floors for banks, featuring very tall ceilings, raised floors and very few columns. 15,000 people work in the building, transported up and down by double-decker elevators. An in-house gallery shows Hong Kong's "history of money," while the library of the Hong Kong Monetary Authority (similar to a central bank) on the 55th floor is publicly accessible. The Airport Express train station "Hong Kong" is located directly underneath the building. On completion, the tower was briefly the tallest skyscraper in the city.

One IFC Two IFC

Exchange Square ⌃⌄
8 Connaught Place, Central
P & T with Remo Riva
1988

PLA Building ⌃»
Lung Wui Road, Admiralty
Pun How Wai
1979

The Exchange Square complex consists of three towers on a common platform with a big bus terminus below. The entrance is on the first upper floor. In addition to the Business Centre, the stock exchange of Hong Kong is also located in the building. The complex is partly owned by Hong Kong Land Corp., the American Club of Hong Kong and the local government. Most tenants are banks and lawyers, plus the consulates of Argentina, Canada and Japan. The tower called One Exchange Square has 52 floors, Two Exchange Square has 51 and Three Exchange Square 32 floors. The band façades of all three towers are clad in glass and pink Spanish granite and have two rounded corners each. The first two towers frame the trading floor of the stock exchange.

This skyscraper with 28 floors is 113 metres tall and located on the grounds of the former Tamar naval base. It is used by the Chinese People's Liberation Army (PLA) as their headquarters in Hong Kong. The building was formerly known as the Prince of Wales Building. The Prince of Wales personally inaugurated it in 1979. Until the handover of the former British crown colony to China in 1997, the building served as headquarters of the British Army in Hong Kong. The name change is based on a decision of the Government in 2000. The tower has the characteristic shape of a chalice to make the building more secure. The upper floors are cantilevered from the central core. Some observers saw an inverted bottle of gin in the shape.

中國人民解放軍駐香港部隊大廈
City Hall Car Park 大會堂停車場
Wilson Parking
TAXI

1

Hang Seng Bank Building ⌃ 016 B
83 Des Voeux Road, Central
Wong & Ouyang
1991

The main building of the Hang Seng Bank, the second largest bank in Hong Kong, has a distinctive aluminium façade with rounded corners. The bank was founded in 1933 and is today part of the British multinational banking and financial services company, HSBC Holdings plc. The Hang Seng Bank Building has 27 floors and is 137 metres tall. The wall panels are six millimetres thick and are as large as an entire floor height. To the north and south, the façade is open in the centre with shimmering green curtain wall mirror glass, while the east and west façades are clad with aluminium panels. Pedestrian bridges on the upper floor lead right into the bank and provide access to the public escalators leading up to the Hong Kong Peak.

World-Wide House » 017 B
19 Des Voeux Road, Central
Wong & Ouyang
1980

World-Wide House is a combined office tower and shopping centre. The site is situated on reclaimed land fill and until 1976 served as the site of the main post office, which was relocated because of the changing water's edge to the north. Underneath the building there is a subway station. The MTR, which operates the subway, bought the site in order to develop it together with the Cheung Kong conglomerate. The 32-storey high-rise tower is well integrated into the pedestrian bridge network of the neighbouring buildings. The shopping centre in the lower three floors (World-Wide Plaza) is organised around an atrium, but it has no natural light. Merchants and buyers from the Philippines, in particular, frequent the mall. In total, the building contains

over 40,000 square metres of floor space. The tower in plan is shaped like two boxes fused together. The column grid relates to the structure of the subway station below and at the same time follows the irregular trapezoid shape of the site. The World-Wide Centre is the precursor of the Admiralty Building, which conceptually and architecturally is almost identical.

Shun Tak Centre

200 Connaught Road
Spence Robinson Architects
1986

018 C

The Shun Tak Centre is an office and transportation complex in Sheung Wan, known as the starting point for ferries to Macau and mainland China. Above a four-storey podium with a shopping centre,

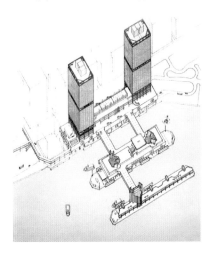

bus terminal, taxi stand and parking garage are placed two 38-storey office towers with rectangular floor plans and the Ferry Terminal with a helipad. Shun Tak Building serves as headquarters of the company of the same name owned by billionaire Stanley Ho, who owns many of the casinos in Macau. The first eastern tower, completed in 1984, is called China Merchants Tower today. Originally, it housed the Hotel Victoria, but it was rebuilt as an office tower. The second, western tower, completed two years later, has its long side parallel to the water and not the short one like the first. The façades of both towers are covered with blue mirrored glass. A bright red painted steel framework interrupts the glass façades. The two jetties have waiting rooms, a customs office, room for the harbour master and immigration offices. Eight boats and catamarans can dock there at the same time. They are arranged parallel to the coast, so that the boats do not have to turn around. The two towers form a symbolic gateway to Hong Kong.

Western Market Hall
323 Des Voeux Road
Tao Ho
1906 / 1991 / 2003

019 C

Man Mo Temple ⌃
124–126 Hollywood Road
Architect unknown
1847

020 C

Western Market Hall is one of the oldest buildings in Sheung Wan and the oldest covered market in the city. Originally it was the northern wing of the main market hall that was knocked down for construction of the Sheung Wan Complex in 1981. The detached building occupies an entire city block. Originally the four-storey hall in an Edwardian style was purely a food market. Since 1990, the hall has been a listed building and in 1991 it was reopened after extensive renovations. The brick walls are striped on all four corners. On the ground floor there are mainly textile traders today and the top floor contains a large restaurant.

A Man Mo Temple is dedicated to the two gods Man Cheong and Mo Tai (or Kwan Tai). These two gods were worshipped in the Ming and Qing dynasties by students who hoped for better results in examinations. The Man Mo Temple in Hollywood Road is the main building of a complex of three structures, which also includes the Lit Shing Temple in 128 Hollywood Road and the Kung So Assembly Hall. Since 1908, the temple has been managed by the charitable organisation Tung Wah Group of Hospitals. Today this temple, the largest Man Mo temple in Hong Kong, is a registered historic landmark.

Li Po Chun Chambers Building   `021` `B`

189 Des Voeux Rd., Sheung Wan
Wong Tung
1995

The Li Po Chun Chambers Building is a 31-storey office tower in the west of Hong Kong Island. Its façade consists of a frameless curtain wall. Since it faces onto an elevated road, sound-proof glass was used. The post-modern forms of the roof and the canopies are made of aluminium panels with the same metallic finish as the walls. The front towards the harbour has horizontal stripes of blue-green mirror glass and granite. Two small towers on the roof are accentuated by masts. The entrance hall is on the third floor, overlooking the neighbouring elevated road towards the sea. The central façade is convex, and all floors are column-free. Only the top two office floors have more generous floor heights than the floors below.

Grand Millennium Plaza

183 Queen's Road, Central
Hsin Yieh Architects & Engineers
1997

The commercial complex Grand Millennium Plaza (also known as COSCO Plaza) was built on a 7,200-square-metre plot of land in Sheung Wan district. More than 100,000 square metres of floor space are housed in a 52-storey and a 28-storey office tower, which frame a plaza that connects Wing Lok Street with Queen's Road.

1

The Center

99 Queen's Road
Dennis Lau & Ng Chun Man
1997

023 B

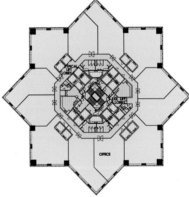

The Center is a skyscraper with a height of 346 metres and 73 floors, currently the fifth-tallest tower in the city. It is one of the few skyscrapers in Hong Kong whose structure consists of a pure steel frame without a concrete core for bracing. Hundreds of neon lights illuminate the Central Tower at night, increasing towards the top at dusk. Their light changes through the whole spectrum of colours. Before Christmas, the neon lights are switched on to show a large Christmas tree. For the building, many small plots of land needed to be merged. The developer, the Land Development Corporation (Urban Renewal Authority since 1999), demolished some old buildings and narrow streets for the tower. Still, the shape of the site is irregular. Many of the traditional clothing stores, which formerly were to be found in the area along Wing On Street, had to be moved to the Western Market.

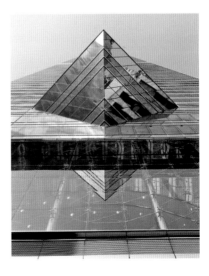

Central Police Station

10 Hollywood Road, Central
Charles St. George Cleverly
1864/1905/1919/1925

024 B

Currently the former police headquarters in Hong Kong is awaiting a new use. The oldest component, a three-storey police station, was built in 1864 next to Victoria Prison. In 1905 one more floor was added to it. It has massive granite staircases and balustrades of iron. In 1880 the ensemble was built around blocks A and B and in 1913 it was extended by blocks C and D and in 1919 the new police headquarters was built on Hollywood Road. The letters "G" and "R" above the doorway refer to the British King George V. The four-storey main building is clad in a late Victorian-style red brick and granite and has a grey-blue façade with Doric columns. In 1925 two-storey stables were built around the parade ground at the rear, which was later used as an armoury. After the Second World War a new police headquarters was built in Wan Chai. Today the former Central Police Station consists of seven buildings that are now all listed monuments. As some of the few preserved buildings of the colonial period in Hong Kong, the former police headquarters will be transformed into a museum and a food plaza. The former prison will become a theatre. Herzog & de Meuron from Basle, Switzerland, will redesign the police headquarters and turn the complex into a private arts and cultural centre. 16 of the 19 historic buildings will be preserved and will be flanked with two new buildings on the west and east sides. The structures are well preserved and need very little intervention to be revitalised.

Government House

Government House

Upper Albert Road, Central
Charles St. George Cleverly
1855/1942

025 B

Government House has traditionally been the official residence of the "Chief Executive" of Hong Kong. It was used as the official residence of the British Governor from 1855 to 1997, over the entire period of British rule over Hong Kong. 25 of the 28 governors lived in this building. Originally it was designed in the colonial style of the Neo-Renaissance by Charles St. George Cleverly (1819–1897), second Surveyor General of Hong Kong. In 1891 an extension was added to accommodate a large ballroom. Government House was used from 1855 to the 1930s by the Legislative Council as well, which from 1891 on met in the ballroom. Under the Japanese occupation of 1941–1945, however, it was substantially reshaped and served the Japanese governor of Hong Kong. Japanese architect Seichi Fujimura added a new tower and roof elements in 1944. After the handover of Hong Kong to China in 1997, Government House was turned into a reception building for ceremonies and banquets. Tung Chee Hwa,

the first Chinese Chief Executive of Hong Kong, lived elsewhere, but Donald Tsang, the second Chief Executive, moved into Government House in 2006. The main entrance is located to the south, facing Victoria Peak. The northern wing has several offices and secretariats. Government House has a small front and a large rear garden with beautiful azaleas. In the ballroom, office, dining- and conference hall receptions are often held. At the main entrance along Upper Albert Road, there are two guardhouses. Since the 1990s the ballroom can be used on three Fridays a month for events by non-profit organisations.

Hong Kong Visual Arts Centre 026 D

7A Kennedy Road, Central
Wong Tung
1992

The Hong Kong Visual Arts Centre (VAC) consists of two historic buildings and one new one at the edge of Hong Kong Park. The oldest building is the Cassels Block, formerly a military barracks for married British officers of the Victoria Barracks. It is a listed building and was supplemented by a new building and connected to an Art-Nouveau-component. A glass arcade links the old and new buildings over six storeys. The VAC is part of the Art Promotion Office in Hong Kong, which is responsible for local artists, and supports their work. It offers nine studios for sculptors, ceramic designers and print artists. There is also an auditorium, a gallery and two multi-functional spaces. The VAC organises workshops, exhibitions, seminars and lectures and has an artist-in-residence programme.

St. John's Cathedral » 027 B

4 Garden Road, Central
Charles St. George Cleverly
1849

St. John's Cathedral is an Anglican church in the diocese of Hong Kong Island, and seat of the Archbishop of Hong Kong. It is the oldest Western ecclesiastical building in Hong Kong and the oldest Anglican Church in East Asia. Since 1996, St. John's Cathedral has been a listed building. In 1941, when the Japanese took over Hong Kong, the church was used as a "Japan Club" and many of the ornaments and stained glass windows were removed. In 1981 Peter Kwong Kong Kit was ordained here as the first Chinese bishop of Hong Kong. Architecturally, the church is a simplified adaptation of the Gothic style. Its bell bears the inscription "VR" on its western face in memory of Queen Victoria. The first pew was reserved for the British Governor of Hong Kong and visiting members of the Royal family.

Hong Kong Club

5 Chater Road, Central
Harry Seidler
1984

028 B

The 25-storey office building that now serves the Hong Kong Club is the third building to house this influential club in the city. Its construction was accompanied by a long controversy. The previous building, constructed in 1897 and designed by Palmer & Turner in the Victorian Neo-Renaissance style, was demolished in 1981 despite vocal protests. The Club, founded in 1846, originally had its three-storey club house on D'Aguilar Street, at its junction with Queen's Road. However, in 1897 the Club moved to a larger plot by the sea, created by the Central Praya land reclamation. In referendums in 1974, 1977 and 1978, Club members voted against demolition and new construction and for the renovation of the existing building. In 1980 the building was listed as a historical monument. Because the fire and structural safety of the old structure was called into question, and to strike capital from a major new building, finally the Club decided to accept the offer of the Hong Kong Land Corp. to take over the demolition and construction costs in exchange for the rental income of the upper floors for 25 years. The Club itself uses the lower four floors (7,400 square metres) in the podium as dining rooms and bars for its members. The 17 upper floors are leased. Since 2009, the building has been solely owned by the Club again. The Club now uses eight floors and the other storeys are rented out.

Bank of China (old building) ⌄ 029 B

2A Des Voeux Road, Central
P & T
1950

The 17-storey old building of the Bank of China was constructed only a year after the Communist Party came to power in China. Intended to be one of the best and largest houses in the city in order to demonstrate the power of the Communist Party, it was deliberately built seven metres taller than the neighbouring building of the private Hong Kong and Shanghai Bank (constructed in 1935, demolished in 1980). The Bank of China building was intended to show Hong Kong citizens an alternative to domination by British colonial masters. In the 1960s, speakers were mounted onto the façade playing Chinese patriotic propaganda. P & T also designed the building of the biggest competitors of the Bank of China, the Hong Kong and Shanghai Bank. In 1998 the interiors of the Bank were fully renovated.

Cheung Kong Centre ⌃ 030 B

2 Queen's Road, Central
Leo A. Daly with César Pelli
1999

This high rise with 62 floors and a height of 283 metres was the third-tallest building in the city at the time of its construction. To make room for it, the site of the former Hilton Hotel (demolished in 1996), the Beaconsfield Houses and a car park that the government sold in 1996 were merged. The Cheung Kong Centre is located between Norman Foster's HSBC building and I. M. Pei's Bank of China Tower. Coloured lights on its sides create an atmospheric illumination at night. The building serves as the corporate Headquarters of Cheung Kong Holdings (CKH) and is managed by its subsidiary, Hutchison Whampoa. Some floors are leased to international banks. Architecturally, the conventional, American design of the building seems nondescript compared to its prominent neighbours. In height it mediates between them. The façades are made of glass sheets (2.4 × 2.1 metres in size) with built-in fiber-optic cables for illumination. The column-free, raised floors are 2,000 square metres in size. The top floor serves the company patriarch Li Ka Shing as his apartment.

Citibank Plaza

 031 B

3 Garden Road, Central
Leo A. Daly with Rocco Design
1992

Citibank Plaza is an office complex consisting of the 50-storey Citibank Tower (205 metres high), the 40-storey ICBC Tower, a three-storey underground car park and a retail podium. The L-shaped high-rise buildings with all-glass façades and 149,000 square metres of space are amongst Hong Kong's largest office buildings. More than 10,000 people work here. Due to its height, Citibank Plaza is one of the most dominant buildings in Central. The lower 26 floors of the towers can be linked together, if tenants want large contiguous areas of up to 3,200 square metres. A ten-storey structural glazing façade brings daylight into the lobby and allows for a visual connection through the lobby. The black glass curtain wall has extruded aluminium profiles and areas of black, polished granite. The slightly curved fronts reflect each other.

St. John's Building
33 Garden Road, Central
KNW Architects + Engineers
1988

032 B

St. John's Building is a skyscraper owned by the Hong Kong and Shanghai Hotels Corp., which also operates the tram to the Hong Kong Peak. It stands next to the base station. Built on a small and steep plot of land, it contains the ground floor of the station. The previous building, St. John's Apartments, was constructed in 1935. In 1964 the reinforced concrete structure with eight apartments and a penthouse was demolished and replaced by a 14-storey office building. It had to make way for the present building with 21 floors. The floor plan is rectangular with rounded edges and also the windows have "rounded corners". The walls of the lobby and railway station, too, are decorated with oval shapes. Columns clad in reflective stainless steel, mirrored windows and aluminium-clad panels complete the façade.

The Landmark

16 Des Voeux Road, Central
P & T/Kohn Pedersen Fox
1980/1983/2006

033 B

The Landmark is a twin tower with a lattice-style façade dating from the early 1980s. The two 44-storey office towers are set at an angle to each other and embrace a plaza. Above an atrium, with its fountain and shopping centre, lies the entrance to offices on the second floor. A pedestrian bridge connects the Landmark towers with the Galleria shopping centre across the street. Originally, the famous Hong Kong Hotel stood on this site. The two towers are called Edinburgh Tower and Gloucester Tower. In addition, there is a third, 14-storey building called York House. In 2003, a part of Edinburgh Tower was redesigned for the Mandarin Oriental Hotel. The shopping centre was extended into the 3rd and 4th floors. This conversion, designed by Kohn Pedersen Fox, was inaugurated in 2006.

Chong Hing Bank Centre
24 Des Voeux Road, Central
P & T
2006

Chong Hing Bank was founded in Hong Kong in 1948. Its new office building in Central was designed by P & T. With its 26 floors, it is one of the smaller high-rises along Des Voeux Road. The glass fa-çade is shaped like a crystal. Previously the headquarters was located in the New World Tower. The 10,000-square-metre building accommodates all central bank-ing functions under one roof, and boasts a double-height main hall onto the street.

Luk Hoi Tong Tower
31 Queen's Road, Central
Rocco Design Architects Ltd.
2011

 035 B

The new high-rise of the Luk Hoi Tong Corp. (LHT) was built on land on which a famous movie theatre stood for fifty years. The new construction offers 21,000 square metres of modern office and retail space as well as restaurants. The tower stands on a prominent street corner in the pedestrian zone Theatre Lane. One of the sides of the folded façade is turned around the podium.

Entertainment Building « ≈
30 Queen's Road, Central
P & T
1993

This postmodern skyscraper combines retail and office spaces. The façades are clad in polished beige Brazilian granite. At the top a neo-Gothic crown adorns a pyramidal roof covered in sheet-metal, which is only visible from a distance. A theatre used to stand on the site and was knocked down to make way for this building. The 34 floors offer 20,000 square metres of rental space. Only the top 26 floors serve as offices. Because of the topography of the site, the entrances are at different levels.

The Centrium »
60 Wyndham Street, Central
DP Architects
2001

The Centrium is an office tower with 41 floors and a height of 189 metres, built above a two-storey retail podium. Overall, it offers 23,700 square metres of floor space. The tip of the antenna was added a year after completion of the building and is colourfully illuminated at night. The Centrium has 25 office and six parking floors, with six express elevators bringing employees to their offices. A garden terrace with fountain is also part of the building.

The Fringe Club ⌃

038 B

2 Lower Albert Road, Central
Danby & Leigh
1890

The Fringe Club is a non-profit cultural institution, which has its headquarters in the former Old Dairy Farm Depot of 1890. The low building was once used as cold storage and has façades of red brick with yellow plaster strips. In 1913 it was turned into a milk shop, a chimney for smoking food and a caretaker's apartment. Until the relocation of the Dairy Farm Corp. in the 1970s, the building served as its corporate headquarters. The Fringe Club bought the empty building in 1984 and converted it into a cultural centre. Today, the building includes two small theatres, three galleries, a pottery workshop, rehearsal rooms, a restaurant and two cafes, a rooftop garden and offices. The building has been declared a National Monument.

General Post Office

2 Connaught Place, Central
K. M. Tseng
1976

039 B

The main building of the Hong Kong Post Office was located directly on the seafront by the ferry pier, because post was usually transported by ship. Due to various land reclamation projects, the building is no longer situated on the waterfront. In 1967 the Hong Kong government intended to construct a tall 30-storey tower on this site, with five floors reserved for the post office and the other floors used as office space. However, the General Post Office building was only allowed to be five floors tall because the neighbouring building, Jardine House, enjoyed the privilege of a clear view of the harbour. Its height is limited to a maximum of 120 feet (40 metres). The General Post Office was the first building in Hong Kong to have a central system for vacuum cleaning.

1

City Hall
5 Edinburgh Place, Central
Ron Phillips and Alan Fitch
1962

040 B

Since Hong Kong is not a city but a national "territory", it has no mayor and no city council. The Town Hall in Hong Kong therefore has a different function: it is a service and cultural centre. It contains a hall in which the Governors of Hong Kong are sworn in. The first town hall (which stood from 1869 to 1933) was located on the site of today's HSBC Bank Main Building and the Bank of China Tower. It was designed by the architect A. Hermite from France. The present town hall was built on a site reclaimed from the sea. The new structure is made of steel and concrete in the style of classic modernism and consists of two buildings that frame a garden: a twelve-storey tower block and a three-storey low-rise building comprising a concert hall with 1,400 seats, three restaurants and a 460-seats-theatre. The entrance to the low building with exhibition space is on the axis of the Queen's Pier. The major public open spaces were intended to be a political statement. Until 2001 the main library of Hong Kong was also located here. The walled memorial garden is dedicated to the war dead of World War II and is often used as a backdrop for wedding photographs.

Land reclamation project between Central and Wan Chai

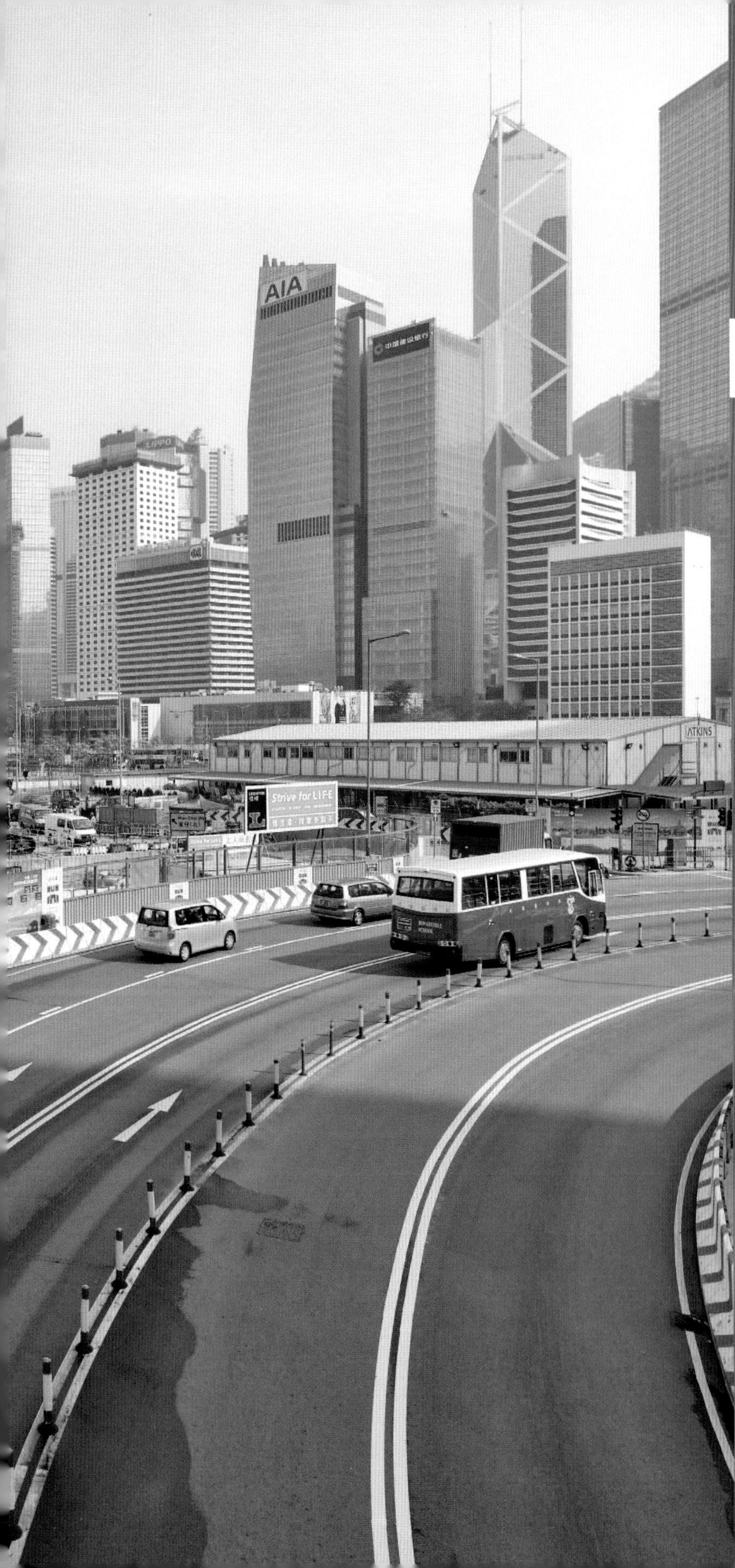
AIA
Strive for LIFE
ATKINS

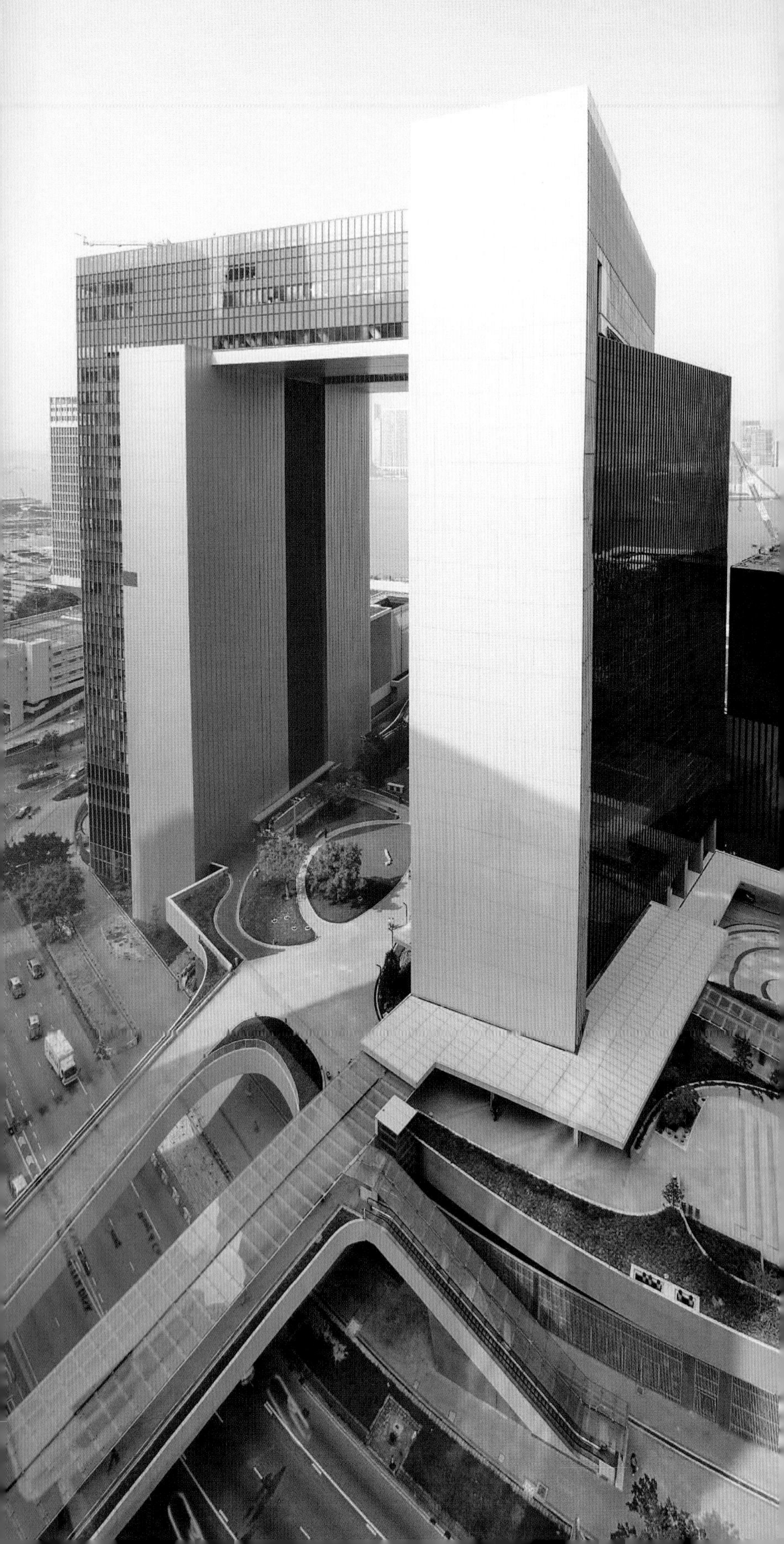

1

Central Government Complex   041 D
1 Legislative Council Road
Rocco Design Architects Ltd.
2011

The new headquarters of the Hong Kong Government was built on the Tamar Site on reclaimed territory. It houses the Office of the Chief Executive, the Parliament (Legislative Council, also called LegCo) and the Central Government offices. The ensemble consists of three parts: two high-rise buildings with 27 (East) and 23 floors (West), which form a gate; a four-storey block containing the Office of the Chief Executive and the Chamber of the Executive Council; and a four-storey LegCo block containing the Chamber and a ten-storey administration building. Parliament Hall was designed in deliberate contrast to its colonial predecessor. The block contains committee rooms, press rooms and the offices of MPs. Green roofs, double façades and a sea-water cooling system help reduce the energy consumption. A green landscape garden winds through the gate, while two wings are set at a slight angle to each other.

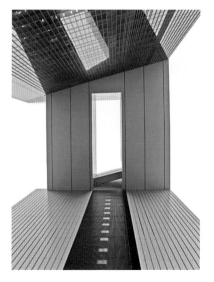

Admiralty Centre ⩔
18 Harcourt Road, Central
Wong & Ouyang
1980

043 D

The 33- and 28-storey twin tower was commissioned by Cheung Kong Holdings. It is more interesting for its urban design than for its architecture: here for the first time a Hong Kong real estate tycoon collaborated with the Hong Kong subway company MTR to economically exploit the favorable location that an underground station creates. The towers stand on a four-storey base with shops directly above the subway station. The podium has closed façades made of white ceramic tiles, and the shopping centre is lit by a skylight. The towers, designed by architectural company Wong & Ouyang, are square in plan with slightly rounded corners and have black curtain walls made of mirror glass. The higher tower is wider than the lower one. Typologically and architecturally the Admiralty Centre resembles the World-Wide House, planned by the same architects for the same client.

Far East Finance Centre ⩘
16 Harcourt Road, Central
Wong & Ouyang
1982

042 D

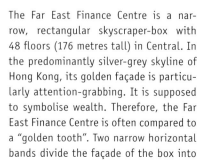

The Far East Finance Centre is a narrow, rectangular skyscraper-box with 48 floors (176 metres tall) in Central. In the predominantly silver-grey skyline of Hong Kong, its golden façade is particularly attention-grabbing. It is supposed to symbolise wealth. Therefore, the Far East Finance Centre is often compared to a "golden tooth". Two narrow horizontal bands divide the façade of the box into three parts.

CITIC Tower

1 Tim Mei Avenue, Admiralty
P&T
1997

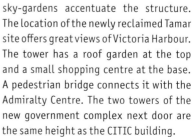

044 D

This building is the headquarters of the CITIC Pacific conglomerate. Located on a triangular site, the 33-storey tower follows the plot shape in plan. Several sky-gardens accentuate the structure. The location of the newly reclaimed Tamar site offers great views of Victoria Harbour. The tower has a roof garden at the top and a small shopping centre at the base. A pedestrian bridge connects it with the Admiralty Centre. The two towers of the new government complex next door are the same height as the CITIC building.

Pacific Place ⌃

88 Queensway, Admiralty

Wong & Ouyang

1988–2004

045 D

Pacific Place is an ensemble of buildings consisting of three office towers and hotels over a large shopping centre with four floors and 130 shops. One Pacific Place comprises the Marriott Hotel and The Upper House, number Two has two luxury hotels and 270 apartments, while Three Pacific Place was completed most recently. It lies outside the site and has an all-glass façade. Pacific Place was built on the site of the former Victoria Barracks and its site has a slope of 26 metres. In addition to two high-rise buildings with a rectangular floor plan (the 40-floor Marriott Hotel and a 36-floor office building), there are also two with an elliptical floor plan: The Conrad Hotel with 36 floors and the Island Shangri-La with 50 floors. They have horizontal mirrored glass façades with white metal panels. The Swire Corp. bought the land and developed the ensemble. A pedestrian bridge leads to the Queensway Plaza and the United Centre. Escalators lead directly to the nearby subway station on one side and Hong Kong Park on the other.

Asia Society ⌃　　046 D
9 Justice Drive, Admiralty
Tod Williams Billie Tsien Architects
2012

British Consulate-General ⌄　　047 D
1 Supreme Court Road, Admiralty
Terry Farrell
1997

The Asia Society was founded by John D. Rockefeller in New York in 1956 to inform Americans about Asian culture. As the first centre of the Asia Society outside the United States, the Asia Society Hong Kong (ASHK) was founded in 1990. Recently four former British military buildings in Admiralty were converted to become its new headquarters. The former explosives depot was re-designed by Tod Williams and Billie Tsien of New York. Three of the buildings are listed monuments. The former military camp had stood empty since the 1980s. The new Hong Kong Centre is only the second building that the Asia Society ever built for itself. The compound consists of the Gallery (Magazine Building A from 1868), the Miller Theatre (Magazine Building B), with a 107-seat auditorium and the Hong Kong Jockey Club Hall for conferences and lectures. The fourth building was formerly used by the military police and currently serves as the administration office of the Asia Society. The visitor centre contains a cafe, a roof garden and a shop. The architects contrasted their horizontal design for buildings only two and a half storeys high with the verticality of Hong Kong. The upper area of the site is connected to the lower entrance pavilion by a double-deck pedestrian bridge.

The heavy, post-modern building of the British Consulate and British Council in Hong Kong is the largest consulate that the UK operates. It is larger than many embassies of Great Britain. It serves Hong Kong, Macao and consular affairs in Taiwan. Because of Hong Kong's special political status, the British Consul reports directly to the Foreign Office in London and not to the Embassy in Beijing. The British Council is located in the other half of the building, which was opened shortly after the consulate. Only the U.S., Malaysia and Indonesia have built stand-alone buildings for their consulates in Hong Kong.

Edward Youde Aviary
Hong Kong Park, Central
Wong Tung & Partners
1991

048 D

The Edward Youde Aviary is Hong Kong's largest aviary. Located in the south of Hong Kong Park, it is one of the largest walk-in aviaries in the world. Visitors walk on an elevated walkway at the level of the treetops, so they can see the birds up close. The aviary is up to 30 metres tall and inhabited by birds from the Malesia region, stretching from Malaysia and the Philippines to Indonesia and New Guinea. The aviary is operated by the city and named in honour of Sir Edward Youde, Governor of Hong Kong from 1982 to 1986. It is 3,000 square metres in size and provides habitat for 800 birds from a hundred different species. The small rectangular entrance building houses an exhibition of birds' eggs. A water area provides a habitat for pelicans. There are three smaller cages. The structure takes advantage of the topography of the steep downhill terrain, on which there were many trees worthy of preservation. A series of three large steel arches carrying a net and a fourth, smaller one forms the entrance.

1

The Peak Tower

128 Peak Road, The Peak
Terry Farrell
1996

049 A

In 1881, Alexander Findlay Smith, who owned a hotel on the peak, began construction of a funicular railway to the mountain top overlooking the city. The railway, with simple wooden terminals at both ends, was officially inaugurated in 1888. Today, the peak tram line is owned by the Hong Kong and Shanghai Hotels Group, which also owns the famous Peninsula Hotel in Hong Kong. In 1972, for the mountain station, a more elaborate building was inaugurated. However it has now been demolished in favour of a fancy new building by British architect Terry Farrell. Today the Peak Tower is not just a train station, but also a leisure and shopping centre. It has more than 10,000 square metres of space over seven floors. As with the previous building, the base and top of the tower are separated by a shaft. Special attention was paid to the shape of the building, which occupies a prominent place in the skyline of Hong Kong. Situated on "Victoria Gap", at an altitude of 396 metres above sea level and thus 156 metres below the Victoria Peak, the "wok" shape of the roof is particularly striking. From the observation deck on the third floor, visitors have stunning views over Victoria Harbour. In the building there are tourist attractions like "Ripley's Believe It or Not! Odditorium", Madame Tussaud's and a "Peak Explorer Motion Simulator". After a renovation in 2006, the viewing platform was moved to the top of the building. Next to the Peak Tower stands the "Peak Galleria" shopping centre.

Tai Yip Building «≳

050 E

141 Thomson Road, Wan Chai
Denton Corker Marshall
2002

On a small plot of land in Wan Chai, only 16 × 20 metres in size, Denton Corker Marshall from Australia have designed two extremely thin "needles". The 30-storey skyscrapers "lean against the core", and vary in height. Together, the two 8 × 8 metre small boxes offer 160 square metres of floor space per storey. The architects wanted the building "to appear off centre so that it can get noticed in the context of its attention-getting neighbouring buildings at all," according to the architects. The façades are clad with flush windows in irregular patterns, alternating with riveted metal panels. The core with four lifts and escape stairs is windowless and black. The tower shaft has no articulated base at ground floorlevel, which gives it the appearance of having been in an extrusion press. Just a simple, two-storey opening with canopy marks the entrance.

2

Hopewell Centre

051 E

183 Queen's Road East, Wan Chai
Gordon Wu (WKMY Ltd.)
1980

The Hopewell Centre was the first tower in Hong Kong to have a circular floor plan. It offers 64 floors of office space, restaurants and shops. The 216-metre tall tower owes its name to the company Hopewell Holdings, which had built the centre and is headquartered there. The chairman of Hopewell and designer of the building, Gordon Wu, has his office on the top floor. At the time of construction, the Hopewell Centre exceeded Jardine House as the highest skyscraper in Hong Kong. It was then the second-tallest building in Asia. Although the main entrance is on the ground floor, the main access to the Hopewell Centre is on the third floor, where there is a large elevator lobby. The site on which the building was constructed is so steep that the rear entrance towards Kennedy Road is located on the 17th floor. The 62nd floor contains a revolving restaurant, which rotates once per hour. The sky lobby on the 56th floor serves as a transfer-level for guests of the restaurants in the 60th and 62nd floors. The white façade mullions have built-in brackets for window cleaners. Urbanistically, the construction led the expansion of the business district to the east.

Central Plaza

Two IFC

HKCEC

Western Tunnel

交通銀行

奇華月餅

2

Police Headquarters

1 Arsenal Street, Wan Chai
HK Architectural Service Dpt.
2004

052 D

The new headquarters of the Hong Kong Police is located in a skyscraper called May House containing 135,000 square metres of office space. It has 47 floors and a height of 206 metres. The name refers to the building that previously stood on the site, which was extended by 20 floors. It is named after Charles May (1818–1879), the first head of the Hong Kong Police Force (1845), who became head of the Hong Kong Fire Brigade in 1868.

Academy for Performing Arts 053 D
1 Gloucester Road, Wan Chai
Simon Kwan
1985

The Hong Kong Academy for Performing Arts (APA) in Wan Chai is a theatre and also a school for the performing arts. It is considered one of the leading academic institutions in East Asia for education and research in the field of theatre, dance, film, television and stage technology. It focuses on both Chinese and Western performance styles. The APA was commissioned by the Hong Kong Jockey Club. Since 1986, an annual International Dance Conference has been held in the building. The rooms are organised around a triangular atrium, and the triangle motif is also reflected in the street façades, which are covered with ceramic tiles. Space frames shape the roof over the amphitheatre and the atrium. The curved shapes of the garden landscaping contrasts with the angular shapes of the building. The ground floor is divided by a centre aisle into two areas: workshops and studios for the students on one side and a large theatre with 1,200 seats, TV- and recording studios on the other side.

Hong Kong Arts Centre ⚑ 054 E
2 Harbour Road, Wan Chai
Tao Ho
1977

The Hong Kong Arts Centre is a non-profit organisation for the performing and visual arts, film, video and education. Its headquarters offers galleries, three theatres, a cinema, conference and rehearsal rooms, a restaurant and studios. Until the 1960s the Town Hall was the only place for contemporary art in Hong Kong. But in 1968 several artists' organisations obtained a 30 × 30-metre plot of land to construct their new cultural centre on land reclaimed from the sea. As only half of the costs were met in donations, construction work had to be temporarily interrupted at one point. The centre is funded in part from the rental income of the top seven floors of office space. The service cores face the two neighbouring buildings. All main spaces are organised around a five-storey, vertical foyer. The large auditorium is shown as a block in the façade above the entrance. The restaurant, however, has a glass façade. A brightly coloured beam holds the parts together, both symbolically and actually. The whole building is constructed

HKCEC ⌄

1 Expo Drive, Wan Chai
Skidmore, Owings & Merrill et al.
1997, 2009

The Hong Kong Convention and Exhibition Centre (HKCEC) was built right in Victoria Harbour on reclaimed land by Skidmore, Owings & Merrill (SOM) in collaboration with Wong & Ouyang. The HKCEC is the extension of a conference centre that had been built on the adjacent plot at the end of the 1980s, with a more stringent architectural language. Through the glass curtain wall (during construction, the largest in the world) the view of conference participants on three sides is of the surrounding harbour. The curved roof is shaped like a tortoise shell. The Hong Kong Convention and Exhibition Centre includes 8,500 square metres of column-free space. A three-storey bridge combines the old and new wings. As part of a second expansion in 2009, another 19,400 square metres of exhibition space were added. Today the centre has six halls with a total of 53,000 square metres of space, two conference halls with 6,100 seats, two theatres with 1,000 seats, 52 smaller conference rooms and seven restaurants. The building was the scene for the "Hong Kong Handover Ceremony", symbolising the end of the British era in 1997.

2

on a triangular geometry. The 193-seat cinema serves screenings and conferences, parties and press conferences. The McAulay Studio has moveable seating and is used for theatre performances and workshops. It has 76–100 seats. The 439-seat Shouson Theatre has two tiers and is designed for major theatre and dance performances, concerts, film screenings and seminars.

Central Plaza ⌃
18 Harbour Road, Wan Chai
Dennis Lau & Ng Chun Man
1992

056 E

Currently Central Plaza, at a height of 374 metres, is the third-tallest building in Hong Kong. When it was inaugurated in 1992, it was the tallest tower in the city and throughout Asia (until 1996). With its 78 floors, Central Plaza trumped the Bank of China Tower. It was the tallest re-inforced concrete building in the world, until it was surpassed by CITIC Plaza, Guangzhou. Noticeable features of Central Plaza are the shape of the building, the illumination of its façade and the fact that it houses the Sky City Church, the highest church in the world. The skyscraper has a triangular plan with capped peaks. At the top there is a pyramid-shaped neon clock. Every 15 minutes the time is indicated by alternating colours of light. An anemometer was installed at the top of the 102-metre-high mast. The office tower is perched above a 30-metre-tall podium. Above this base there are 57 office floors with a sky lobby and five mechanical floors in between. At the top of the tower there are six more mechanical floors. A public plaza in front of the building covers 8,400 square metres and boasts a garden, fountains and trees. At ground floor level three pedestrian bridges connect the building with the nearby underground station, the congress and exhibition centre and the nearby China Resources Building. The builders got a 20% floor area bonus on the plot, which was reclaimed from the sea. Originally a steel structure was planned, but after a cost analysis the decision was made to use high-strength concrete. By using a climbing formwork, the

construction time could be shortened to that of a steel structure. To allow more offices to overlook the harbour, the three peaks of the triangular floor plan have been cut off. The column-free floor plans are 9 to 13 metres deep. The supply shaft in the centre is also triangular in plan. The office floors have a clear height of only 2.60 metres. The sky lobby on the 46th floor is publicly accessible.

Sun Hung Kai Centre ⌃
30 Harbour Road, Wan Chai
Sun Hung Kai Architects
1981

057 E

The Sun Hung Kai Centre is the headquarters of Sun Hung Kai Properties Corp., one of the leading property companies in Hong Kong. The tower has load-bearing façades filled in with black glass. It has a simple rectangular plan without restraints and cut corners highlighted with white façade elements. The building is 215 metres tall and has 53 floors. The ground floor contains shops and there are restaurants on the second floor.

China Online Centre »

058 E

333 Lockhart Road, Wan Chai
Rocco Design Architects Ltd.
2000

The China Online Centre is an office building in Wan Chai with 52 storeys. The tower
is 201 metres tall and has 16,000 square
metres of floor space. Floors 3 to 17 are
used for parking. This has the advantage that the office floors above (starting from the 22nd floor) get a glimpse of
Victoria Harbour. The top of the tower is
crowned by a billboard.

Times Square Building ⌄

059 F

1 Matheson Street
Wong & Ouyang
1994

Times Square is the name of a double
office tower with 33 and 26 floors and a
14-storey shopping centre, built on the
site of a former tram depot. After the
tram company had been bought by a
real estate tycoon, the city approved
the relocation of the depot to Sai Wan
Ho and Sai Ying Pun and the development of this area. Times Square has
more than 83,000 square metres of retail
space on nine floors, making it the first
"vertical mall" in Hong Kong, which also includes four cinemas. The two office
towers are called Shell Tower and Tower
One and—in a typical postmodern fash-
ion—have heavy stone façades. Extra-
long escalators take guests and tenants
from the lower to the upper floors. In
a contract with the city, the builder
agreed to leave 3,000 square metres
open to the public, but did not follow the
agreement and started to rent out this
space too, resulting in a fine. Tunnels
connect the building to the nearby subway station.

2

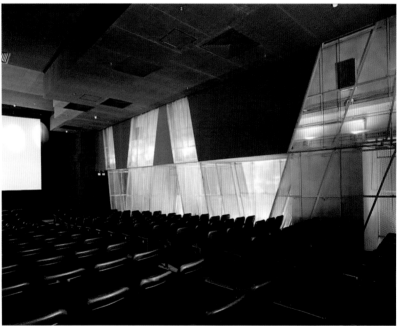

Lee Theatre Plaza Building   060 F

99 Percival Street, Causeway Bay
Wong & Choy
1995

The Lee Theatre Plaza Building stands on the site occupied by the famous Lee Theatre from 1927. Peking operas and films were shown in the old theatre, owned by the Hysan family. It was demolished in 1991 to make way for a new building with office and retail space. The new

Lee Theatre Plaza does include a cinema, but otherwise the design by Wong and Choy is not too reminiscent of Art Deco theatres of the 1920s. The skyscraper with 22 floors is 131 metres tall. The post-modern building has cupolas on its rounded street corner: both at the arcade, which frames the entrance on the corner, and at the top of the tower, they mark the three-storey atria below. The cinema has a bright blue foyer and halls, while its walls are covered in perforated metal.

Manulife Plaza ⌄
061 F

33 Hysan Avenue, Causeway Bay
Dennis Lau
1997

The Manulife Plaza Building is situated in the west of Causeway Bay. It has a height of 240 metres and 52 storeys. The tower is triangular in plan, and is owned by a Canadian insurance company called Manulife. For its construction, the Lee Gardens Hotel, which was previously located on the site, was demolished. The new building is therefore sometimes referred to as Lee Gardens. On two of its broadsides the Manulife Plaza Tower is oriented towards the city. One leg of the triangle is oriented towards Victoria Harbour. There are bay windows at the building's corners.

2

Cubus Building ⌃
062 F

1–3 Hoi Ping Road, Causeway Bay
Woods Bagot
2010

The 25-storey office tower of the Cubus Building and its built-in lighting are inspired by melting ice cubes: geometrically bent polygons shape the entire ice-blue glittering glass façade of the tower. At night, lighting effects add to the expressive design of the building. The Cubus Building offers 5,600 square metres of retail and office space. At several points in the complex there are open decks in different sizes. As a "vertical retail building of a new type", here the typology of a podium-tower was turned into a vertical position. Shoppers who take one of the glass elevators to the upper floors are offered great views of the surrounding cityscape. The name "Cubus" is supposed to be reminiscent of cubism.

Happy Valley Race Course
The Peak
Hopewell Centre
Hong Kong Stadium

Hong Kong Stadium
So Kon Po, Wan Chai
HOK Sport
1953 and 1994

063 F

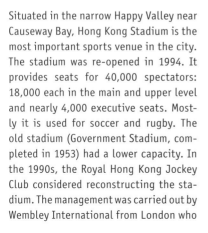

Situated in the narrow Happy Valley near Causeway Bay, Hong Kong Stadium is the most important sports venue in the city. The stadium was re-opened in 1994. It provides seats for 40,000 spectators: 18,000 each in the main and upper level and nearly 4,000 executive seats. Mostly it is used for soccer and rugby. The old stadium (Government Stadium, completed in 1953) had a lower capacity. In the 1990s, the Royal Hong Kong Jockey Club considered reconstructing the stadium. The management was carried out by Wembley International from London who mainly wanted to earn money by running cultural and entertainment events at the stadium. But due to noise complaints from local residents, the stadium may not be used for concerts. In 1998 the contract was therefore dissolved. Two large arched beams span 270 metres along on the field. Three-quarters of seats are covered with a teflon-coated fibreglass fabric, which is impressively illuminated at dusk. Ancillary areas such as locker rooms, mechanical and administration rooms are located partially underground. Currently a new stadium is being planned in South East Kowloon. After its completion, the Hong Kong Stadium will be demolished and the site will be used for more residential skyscrapers.

Manulife Plaza

Western Tunnel

Cross-Harbour Tunnel

AIA Building

064 E

1 Stubbs Road, Causeway Bay
P & T
1967

The building of the American International Assurance Corp. (AIA) stands a short
distance from Victoria's business district. With 21 floors, it looks like a modern white sculpture against the backdrop
of the green hills of Hong Kong Island. To
keep the floors column-free the slabs were
made of post-tensioned concrete carried by an exo-skeleton, a structure outside the façade. A large projecting canopy marks the main entrance. There are
four floors for parking in the basement.
Bronze-coloured windows behind the
framework are shaded by the structure.

Highcliff and The Summit

41 D Stubbs Road, Happy Valley
Dennis Lau & Ng Chun Man
2003

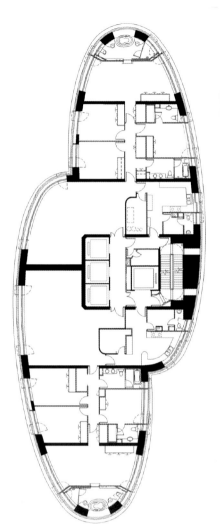

On a steep hillside above Happy Valley, two spectacularly tall and thin residential buildings are placed next to each other on a common platform. The two towers stand close together and are popularly known as the "chopsticks". The 252-metre-tall Highcliff Tower, with 75 floors, is the tallest residential building in Hong Kong. Because of its extreme thinness, a water tank had to be installed at its top as a counterweight, to prevent strong movement in the event of a typhoon. Its floor plan is made of two staggered ovals with only two apartments per floor, each with five rooms. At the intersection of the two ovals lies the core, housing four lifts and escape stairs. The 34th and 57th floors have roofdecks for egress. The top three floors contain mechanical equipment. The adjacent Summit Building has a butterfly-shaped floor plan, with the elevators leading directly into homes. The horizontal strip façades are made of glass, while the nine-storey podium offers parking, a lobby and a swimming pool.

2

AIA Tower North Point

066 G

183 Electric Road, North Point
P & T with Andrew Lee King Fun
1999

This 44-storey skyscraper for the AIA Corp. is 180 metres tall. It faces the former clubhouse of the Royal Hong Kong Yacht Club along Oil Street. The building was commissioned by the Henderson Land Development Corp. Although the the tower offers speculative office space, it was named after the American International Assurance, a former member of the American International Group (AIG). The AIA Tower has its own swimming pool and fitness centre.

One Island East «

067 H

14–18 Westlands Road, Taikoo
Wong & Ouyang
2008

With its height of almost 300 metres the One Island East (OIE) skyscraper dominates the silhouette of the new town East Island in Taikoo. It offers 69 floors of office space. The 37th and 38th floors contain a sky lobby, which is served by six express elevators. On top there are 28 other elevators. The OIE is the sixth high-rise in Hong Kong that is more than a thousand feet tall. Earlier on the site was occupied by the Melbourne Industrial Building and the Aik San Factory Building, but both structures were demolished. The Swire Properties Corp. has its headquarters on the 64th floor. In 2008, the year of completion, a tropical storm has caused some elements of the glass façade to fall to the ground; however fortunately no one was injured. The curtain wall is designed so that it looks as if it was peeled away at the corners. The OIE does not have a traditional podium base, but opens up towards the east with a transparent glass façade facing a plaza with a fountain.

2

Cambridge House

TaiKoo Place

068 H

Island East
Wong & Ouyang
1979–2003

TaiKoo Place is a new town in Quarry Bay, which has been developed since the late 1980s on the grounds of the former Taikoo sugar refinery. The ten new office buildings comprise the Devon House (1993), Dorset House (1994), PCCW Tower (1994), Warwick House (1979), Cornwall House (1984), Somerset House (1988), Lincoln House (1998), Oxford House (1999), Cambridge House (2003), and One Island East (2008). The highest structure is the One Island East tower. All commercial buildings are connected with each other and with the nearby subway station through an air-conditioned pedestrian level. TaiKoo Place is host to many firms involved in advertising and IT, including IBM and PCCW. It has even has more IT firms than the Cyberport. The architects who came up with the urban design plan for the site, Wong & Ouyang, also run their own head office in TaiKoo.

Lincoln House

Oxford House

One Island East

2

PCCW Tower

Dorset House

Cambridge House

Devon House

Sea—their rents are amongst the highest in the city. The stepped roof line follows the silhouette of the mountains in the background. Three cuts open the façade creating roof terraces for the residents and their guests.

Murray House ⌄
Stanley Plaza, Stanley
Aldrich and Collinson
1846

070 A

Named after Sir George Murray, the British Master-General of the Ordnance during its construction, Murray House is a colonial building from the Victorian era, which originally used to stand in Central and served the officers of the Murray Barracks. Its stone walls have flat arched openings on the ground floor and a circular porch with Doric and Ionic columns on the upper floor to facilitate natural ventilation in the subtropical climate. The structure was designed by Aldrich & Collinson of the Royal Engineers, and is one of the oldest public buildings in Hong Kong from the early days of the British mandate. During Japanese occupation of Hong Kong, Murray House was used as the headquarters of the military police. After the Second World War it was occupied by the Government of Hong Kong. In 1982 it was demolished to make room for the new Bank of China. More than 3,000 components have been numbered and catalogued and moved to facilitate its reconstruction in Stanley in 2002. From 2005 to 2013 Murray House served as a maritime museum.

Repulse Bay Apartments
109 Repulse Bay Road
Anthony Ng Architects
1989

069 A

From the beach of Repulse Bay, the Repulse Bay Complex is not to be overlooked. Eight residential towers and a shopping centre with restaurants and medical centre were built on the grounds of the former Repulse Bay Hotel, which stood here from 1920 to 1982. The residential tower blocks are owned by the Peninsula Hotel Company. The hotel has been reconstructed. The architecture of the residential high-rise building with its façade in white and pastel colours and curved shapes recalls the Art Deco style of Miami Beach. All apartments afford a view of the beach and the South China

Cyberport

100 Cyberport Road, Pok Fu Lam
Arquitectonica et al.
2004

071 A

The Cyberport complex is a business incubator for companies in the field of creative digital content, information and communication technology. It was founded and is owned by the state. Designed by the US based practice Arquitectonica with Wong Tung & Partners and The Jerde Partnership, Cyberport includes four office buildings and a five-star hotel, shops and 2,800 homes. Situated on a 24 hectare site at Telegraph Bay, its 100,000 square metres of office space are occupied by over a hundred companies. The complex is made up of a series of interconnected buildings developed in a zigzag pattern along the coast. An internal IT Road leads from the residential area at one end to the hotel and office areas at the other end, which in turns are linked to the technology labs, recreational rooms, seminar and conference and multimedia rooms, a library, a Web-TV studio, a fitness centre, cafes, lounges and bars. The offices can be flexibly expanded horizontally and vertically. A Cyber Centre offers shops and entertainment as well as a garden terrace overlooking a lake.

2

3 **Kowloon**

Bank of China

Cheung Kong Centre

HSBC

3

Star Ferry Pier Tsim Sha Tsui

Salisbury Road, Tsim Sha Tsui
Hung Yip Chan
1957

072 I

Founded in 1888, Star Ferry connects Hong Kong Island and Kowloon, with scheduled trips across Victoria Harbour. Today twelve ferry boats carry about 70,000 passengers daily on two routes (Central to Tsim Sha Tsui and Wan Chai to Tsim Sha Tsui). The main route connects Central with Tsim Sha Tsui. The first pier was built in 1906 at Salisbury Road, but in the same year was destroyed by a typhoon. In 1957, the "twin-pier terminal" with two piers on both sides of the harbour was inaugurated. The terminals are painted green and white like the boats and are designed for 55 million passengers per year. Until the opening of the Harbour Tunnel in 1972, the Star Ferry was the only transport link between Hong Kong and Kowloon. The Pier at Edinburgh

Place with its famous clock tower was built on reclaimed land near town hall and the main post office. The architect of the Star Ferry piers, Hung Yip Chan, worked from 1952 to 1957 in the architectural bureau of the City. His boss, Michael Wright, had added the clock tower. The clock was a gift from John Keswick, who had in turn received it from the Belgian Prince. In 2006 the ferry service was discontinued at this pier and the pier was pulled down, with Piers 7 and 8 on the newly reclaimed site taking over the traffic. The demolition was accompanied by strong protests by preservationists, the Chamber of Architects and the public. Adjacent Queen's Pier was also demolished. The new piers are referred to as "Piers of the third generation": the first generation dated from 1890 (stations included Chater Road) and the second from 1912 the piers on Pedder Street. Since the relocation the number of passengers has fallen sharply.

Hong Kong Space Museum

3

Cultural Centre ⩘

10 Salisbury Rd., Tsim Sha Tsui
Architecural Services Department
1980

The Hong Kong Cultural Centre is located at the southern tip of Tsim Sha Tsui and its sloping roofs are a distinctive landmark of Kowloon. It was built on the site of the former Kowloon Train Station. The multifunctional centre offers a large hall with 2,019 seats in an oval arrangement with two tiers and fine oak panelling. The acoustics can be controlled by means of a mobile sound ceiling and fabric curtains. The Hong Kong Cultural Centre is home to the Hong Kong Philharmonic Orchestra. Its organ, the largest in Asia, was built in Austria. The big theatre next door has 1,734 seats in three tiers. Two large halls are situated at right angles to the foyer in the middle. The Studio Theatre has flexible seating and can accommodate up to 496 people. There also is a gallery and eleven rehearsal rooms. The façades are almost completely closed and clad in pink ceramic tiles. At the base there is a pedestrian arcade.

3

Space Museum ⌃

10 Salisbury Road, Tsim Sha Tsui
Joseph Ming-Gun Lee, Public Works
Dpt., Hong Kong Government
1980

Hong Kong's museum for astronomy and space science was born out of the city's wish for a space museum after it had purchased a planetarium from the Carl Zeiss company in 1974. The building has an east and a west wing. The east wing of the building accommodates the planetarium with a large egg-shaped dome covering 8,000 square metres of floor space:

the Stanley Ho Space Theatre, the Hall of Space Science, workshops and offices. The west wing contains the Hall of Astronomy, an auditorium and the museum shop.

Hong Kong Museum of Art ⌄

10 Salisbury Road, Tsim Sha Tsui
Public Works Dpt., HK Government
1991

This is Hong Kong's most important art museum. Its collections contains approximately 15,800 art objects. The museum was founded by the city in 1962 and was originally located at City Hall.

The Peninsula Hotel
Salisbury Road, Tsim Sha Tsui
W. D. Goodfellow
1928

076 I

The Peninsula ist one of the most famous and oldest hotels in the city. The 300-room building is H-shaped in plan and has repeatedly been voted in polls as the "Best Hotel in the World", partly because its location at the southern tip of Kowloon provides excellent views of Hong Kong Island. In the past the hotel also had its own private pier for incoming ships. The building was the scene of the surrender of the British against Japan in 1941 when they annexed Hong Kong, as this agreement was signed on the third floor of the Hotel. Under Japanese rule the building was renamed Hotel Toa. In 1994 a 30-storey extension in a tempered postmodern style was erected behind the old building. The atrium with drive-up, the façade and lobby of the original structure were kept. Ten floors of the new building are occupied by offices and shops.

3

Kowloon Shangri-La
64 Mody Road, Tsim Sha Tsui
Wong & Ouyang
1981

078 I

Kowloon's Shangri-La Hotel is one of two hotels of this chain in Hong Kong. The building offers views of Victoria Harbour and the Hong Kong skyline on the other side. It contains 720 rooms, four restaurants and several ballrooms. The height of 16 floors was imposed by the flight path of the planes approaching and landing at former Kai Tak Airport. The rooms are situated on a two-storey podium and have bay windows. They are organised in an asymmetrical U-shaped floor plan. The closed parts of the façades are covered with dark green granite.

Old Station Clock Tower
Salisbury Road, Tsim Sha Tsui
Arthur Benison Hubback
1915

077 I

Tsim Sha Tsui was once the terminus of the Kowloon – Canton Railway. Today the clock tower is the only part of the former station, completed in 1915, which has stood the test of time. The station was demolished in 1978 when the rail traffic was moved to the new Hung Hom Station. In its place, the Space Museum and Cultural Centre were built. The 44 metre tall tower now stands alone in the courtyard of the Cultural Centre.

View from *The Peninsula Hotel* to Hong Kong Island

Park Lane Shopper's Boulevard 079 I

Nathan Road, Tsim Sha Tsui
Rocco Design Partnership
1985

Nathan Road is regarded as Hong Kong's most famous shopping street. In its middle section, it forms the eastern edge of Kowloon Park which acted as a break in the urban context before the Park Lane Shopper's Boulevard, a thin strip of shops, was built. The 370-metre-long storefront, which is framed in white aluminium panels, is interrupted only by two entrances to the park. The Park Lane Shopper's Boulevard has been designed by the famous local architect Rocco Yim and is probably the longest building in Hong Kong.

3

Science Museum
2 Science Museum Road, TST
P & T
1990

080 I

Hong Kong's Science Museum offers 18 galleries ranging in topics from light to sound, electricity, magnetism, mathematics, geography and meteorology to transport. Opposite the building there are two small squares, connected by a large staircase. The four-storey museum offers 65,000 square metres of space, an auditorium with 300 seats, a conference room, a laboratory, a shop and a cafeteria. The façades are covered with pink tiles. A turquoise frame depicts the interior on the façade, the columns and beams are shown as grey.

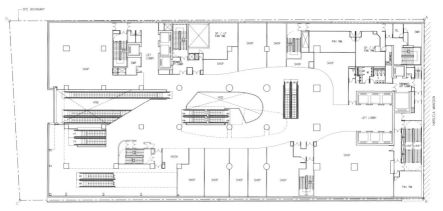

iSQUARE

081 I

63 Nathan Road, Tsim Sha Tsui
Rocco Design and Benoy
2009

The iSQUARE is a huge shopping centre in Kowloon. After the relocation of the Hyatt Regency Hotel architect Rocco Yim re-designed the building as a entertainment and retail complex with various shops, restaurants, five cinemas and the iTower with 31 floors on 56,000 square metres of space. The retail spaces range from the lower to the 8th floor, and are organised around a "sky atrium". The building's elaborate media façade is illuminated at night so that "it can stand up against the neon extravaganza of Nathan Road," according to the architect.

3

The Masterpiece

082 I

18 Hanoi Road, Tsim Sha Tsui
Leo A. Daly
2009

The new focal point of Kowloon is the Masterpiece high-rise building with a height of 261 metres. Above a six-storey shopping centre called K11, integrating elements of art, culture and nature, on floors 3 to 24 is located a Hyatt Hotel with 384 rooms. Floors 27 to 67 offer space for 345 1- to 4-bedroom apartments measuring between 80 and 200 square metres in size. There are both rental apartments and condominiums. The building is located directly above subway station Tsim Sha Tsui overlooking Victoria harbour. Two hollow floors divide the vertical tower, whose's roof resembles an obscure helmet in shape.

Sorrento   The Cullinan   The Arch   ICC Tower

3

The Cullinan

 083 J

6 Union Square, Kowloon
Wong & Ouyang with P & T
2009

Part of the new town above new Kowloon
Station is The Cullinan, a double residential tower on Union Square. It offers some
the most expensive homes in the world.
Currently the north and south towers are
the tallest residential high-rise buildings
in the city (68 floors, 270 metres). The
apartments overlook Victoria harbour.
The name of the tower is derived from a
600-gram diamond that in South Africa
in 1905. The complex houses the W Hotel
in the south tower and the Harbour View
Place Suite with furnished apartments in
the north tower, while the podium contains many shops. To give the building
an "address", small forecourts were cut
away from the podium. Forty-metre-high
glass cases highlight the entrances to the
hotel and the Serviced Apartments architecturally. The roof of the podium is also
used as a driveway. The glass curtain
walls are similar to the ICC office tower
next door.

The Arch

 084 J

1 Austin Road West, Kowloon
Sun Hung Kai Architects
2006

The Arch is a high-rise apartment building with 81 floors and a height of
231 metres, making it Hong Kong's third-
tallest residential building. The structure consists of four towers, the Sun
Tower, Star Tower, Moon Tower and Sky
Tower. The Sun Tower and Moon Tower
are joined together from the 69th floor
on by a club house to form the epony-
mous Arch.

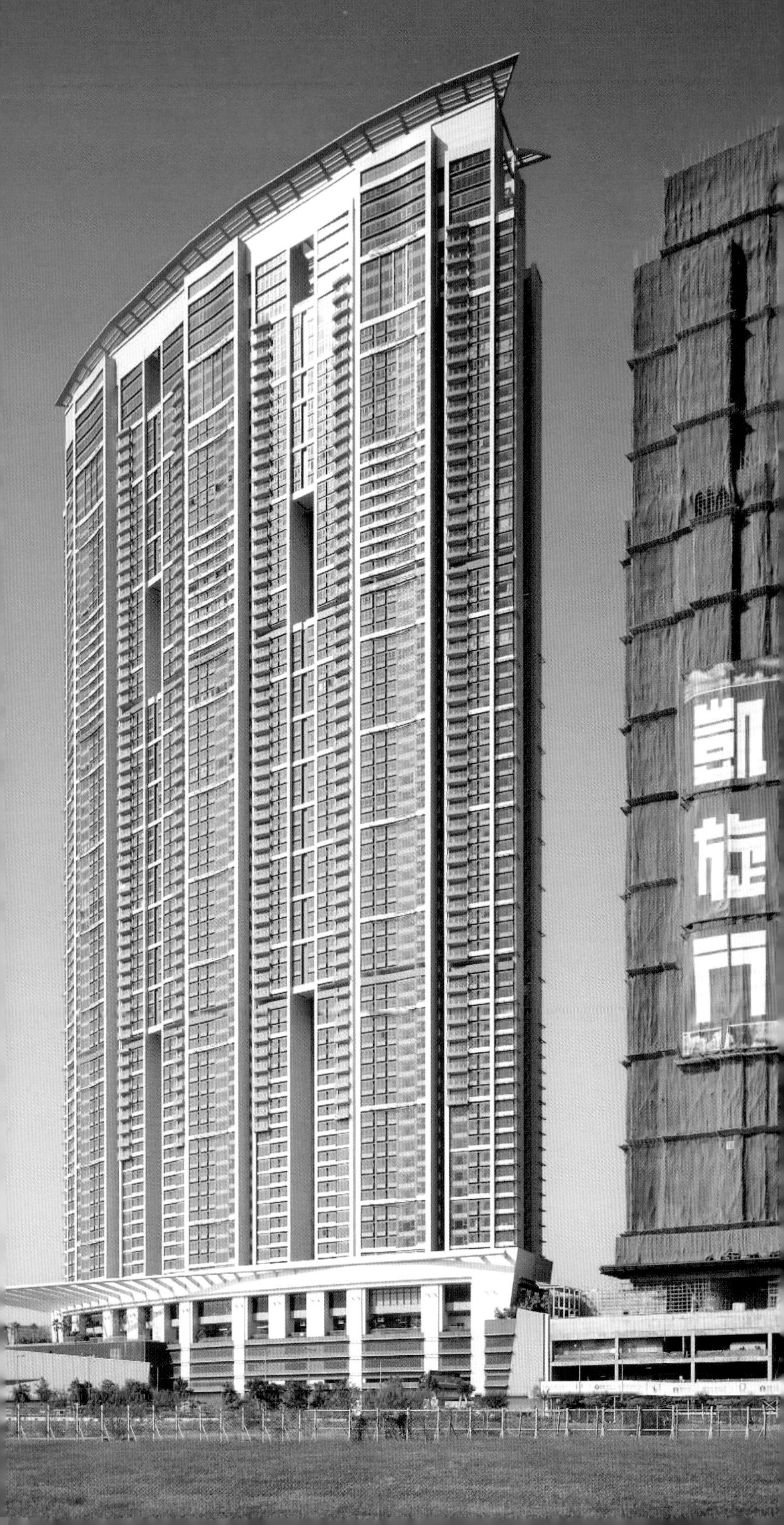
凱旋門

3

ICC Tower ⌃

085 J

1 Austin Road, West Kowloon
Kohn Pedersen Fox
2010

Currently the International Commerce Centre (ICC) with 118 floors is the highest tower in the city and the fifth-tallest skyscraper in the world. It was designed by the New York office of Kohn Pedersen Fox (KPF). The 484-metre tall tower belongs to "Union Square" development above Kowloon Station. It was built in phases between 2007 and 2010. Owners are MTR Corporation and Sun Hung Kai Properties. Originally, the tower was intended to be even taller. The structure contains a hotel, a viewing platform, offices, shops and a garage. The tower of the Ritz Carlton Hotel was inaugurated in 2011. The hotel is situated on the 102nd to 118th floors and contains the world's tallest bar and the swimming pool. A 2,800 square metre suite is located on the 107th floor. From the lobby in the 9th floor express elevators take guests to the sky lobby on the 103rd floor in only 50 seconds, 425 metres above the street. Three floors below, there is a public observation deck.

The Harbourside «

086 J

1 Austin Road West, Kowloon
P & T
2004

The Harbourside building is a triple residential tower constructed on reclaimed new land in West Kowloon. It belongs to the Union Square complex around the new Kowloon Station. With a height of 255 metres and 74 floors, it is extremely high. It is one of the one hundred tallest buildings in the world. The three towers are joined at their base, in the middle and at the top. This was done for two reasons: first, to not appear as a gigantic residential wall and secondly the gaps help reduce the wind pressure in case of a typhoon.

Teaching Hotel ICON

17 Science Museum Rd., Kowloon
Rocco Design Architects Ltd.
2011

The former residence hall of the Poly-
technic University was rebuilt and turned
into a "catering school teaching hotel".
In addition to the 262 guest rooms for
teaching staff, it also continues to maintain classrooms in the "hotel". Glass
atriums spatially and visually connect
the two ends of the site on several levels.

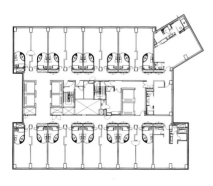

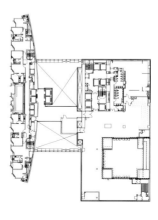

Hung Hom Station ⌃
8 Cheong Wan Road, Hung Hom
Norman Foster
1998

088 K

Hong Kong Coliseum ⌄
9 Cheong Wan Road, Hung Hom
Urban Council
1983

089 K

The Hung Hom Railway Station serves the rail link from Hong Kong to mainland China. Because of the ever-increasing passenger volume the existing train station of 1974 (Kowloon Station then) became too small. Lord Norman Foster from London designed a pavilion-style extension to the east, which doubles the floor space. A shed roof and glass walls allow daylight to penetrate deep into the main hall. Hung Hom is the southern terminus of East Rail Line and West Rail Line and the cross-border links. The new station is designed to accommodate 500 trains a day.

The Hong Kong Coliseum is a multi-purpose arena with 12,500 seats. Belonging to the the Ministry of Culture, it is the second largest hall in Hong Kong after AsiaWorld-Arena. In addition to the main arena, it also offers a range of conference and reception rooms. The building is shaped like an inverted pyramid with a side length of 41 metres. If necessary, the concrete floor can be covered with a variety of surfaces, platforms and equipment. A four-sided display screen in the centre of the hall shows events in the arena to all guests. The arena is usually used for congresses, live

3

television broadcasts and graduation ceremonies, but even ice skating competitions or beauty contests can be held in the Coliseum.

The Harbourfront Landmark
11 Wan Hoi Street, Kowloon
Dennis Lau & Ng Chun Man
2001

This skyscraper with its 70 floors and a height of 233 metres consists of three towers placed on a seven-storey retail podium. It is conveniently located at the southern tip of Kowloon, overlooking Victoria Harbour. A club in the seventh floor offers a pool which serves the 320 apartments above. The façades are made of glass.

Lok Fu Shopping Centre ⌃   091 M

Wang Tau Hom East Rd., Kowloon

Rocco Design Architects Ltd.

1991

The extension of Lok Fu Shopping Centre is situated on the corner of Wang Tau Hom East Road and Junction Road. On seven floors, it offers 10,000 square metres of space. It is well connected to the public transportation system: an underground station and bus terminus are located right in the building. The vertical circulation is organised around an atrium, which is supplied by natural light from above. The structure and the supply lines were left visible. In front of the shopping centre, there is a public square with shaded seating. The building was commissioned by the Hong Kong Housing Authority.

Run Run Shaw Media Centre »   092 L

18 Tat Hong Avenue, Kowloon

Daniel Libeskind

2011

American-Jewish architect Daniel Libeskind designed the new Run Run Shaw Creative Media Centre of the City University of Hong Kong. The nine-storey structrure is home to media labs, a theatre and classrooms for the Faculties of Engineering and Computer Technology. The centre culminates in many sharp angles and offers rooms for seminars, a multipurpose theatre, exhibit space, a café and a restaurant. Its crystalline body alludes to the Chinese characters for creativity, which is made up of the characters for plow and blade. The media centre was opened in 2011.

Tsuen Wan Columbarium

093 A

Cemetery Road, Kowloon
Dennis Lau
1987

The scarcity of land that characterises Hong Kong seems to continue even after death: instead of using large areas for cemeteries, most of the dead are cremated and their urns kept in multi-storey columbaria. Twice a year, in occasion of the Ching Ming in April and Chung Yeung Festival in October, relatives go there to commemorate their dead. The columbarium built in Tsuen Wan by Dennis Lau is an extreme example of a house of the dead on a small plot. It has ten storeys and follows the topography of its hillside location with terraces and cantilevers. In the lower three floors there are 2,000 family niches and in the seven floors above more than 26,000 further smaller niches. A six-storey atrium with natural light on both sides leads to the grave sites. It is decorated with large murals. The building also has four underground floors.

Broadcasting Centre

70 Pak To Ave., Clearwater Bay
Dennis Lau
1991

The broadcasting centre's building sits alone in the hills of Clearwater Bay. Former Star TV (JC Studio today) was the first satellite TV channel in Hong Kong and is part of the Murdoch Media Group. The building welcomes visitors with a two-storey hall with structural glazing.

Dennis Lau used basic shapes of geometry for his collage-like structure: a pavilion square in plan, supporting a triangular glass roof for example. The main building has three floors and walls clad in grey ceramic tiles. In addition to the two studios, the broadcasting centre contains offices spaces, meeting rooms and synchronisation facilities.

ATL Logistic Centre, Kwai Chung Container Terminal

ATL Logistics Centre

095 A

Berth 3, Kwai Chung Terminal
Dennis Lau
1992

The ATL Logistics Centre is a huge container terminal with a floor area of 900,000 square metres and is considered the largest industrial building in the world. The logistics hub consists of two parts: Centre "A" with seven floors and Centre "B" with 13 floors. In each storey up to four containers can be stacked on top of each other. Approximately 8,000 trucks travel in and out of the building over a three-lane ramp each day. There are more than 1,700 loading bays.

Panda Hotel «

096 N

3 Tsuen Wah Street, Tsuen Wan
Hopewell Construction Company
1992

With 1,026 guest rooms, four-star Panda Hotel in Tsuen Wan is the largest hotel in the New Territories district. The hotel belongs to Hopewell group and is strategically positioned at the city's entrance when coming from the airport. The narrower side of the hotel's divinely simple architecture is decorated with a huge image of climbing pandas. A shopping mall and a park are located in direct vicinity.

Hong Kong Design Institute 097 A

3 King Ling Road, Tseung Kwan O
Coldefy & Associés
2012

The new Hong Kong Design Institute (HKDI) consists of a square platform, four towers and a square-shaped cantilever (100 × 100 metres in size). A concrete, glass and white steel construction featuring a diamond pattern, the "dia-grid", create its striking look. French architects Coldefy & Associés had won the competition for the new HKDI in 2006: this was their first project in Hong Kong. Although HKDI offers 42,000 square metres of floor space for 4,000 media, art and design students, the huge building looks small when compared to the surrounding residential towers in Tseung Kwan. The landscaped plateau anchors an "urban base" with the public space and provides direct access to a nearby subway station. A 60 metre long escalator brings students into the interior and directs them over the upper level into one of the four towers. Seminar rooms, lecture halls, libraries and offices can be found in this "Sky City". The mid-plane contains a gymnasium and sports grounds, a park and the cafeteria. Diagonal in plan, the escalator takes on the structure of the diamond grid. The architects celebrate the circulation architecturally.

Prince of Wales Hospital

098 A

30–32 Ngan Shing Street, Sha Tin
Wong & Ouyang
1984

The State Hospital is part of the Chinese
University of Hong Kong. It is named
after the Prince of Wales, who had inaugurated the hospital himself in 1984. The
hospital has 1,360 beds and 4,000 employees. It serves the eastern and northern New Territories with Shatin, Tai Po
and Sai Kung. The hospital was expanded
to a design by architectural bureau
Wong & Ouyang, who had also designed
the original structure.

Pearl River Necklace Bridge 099 A

Chek Lap Kok/Macau
NL Architects
construction date unclear

4

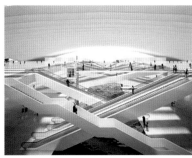

This giant bridge across Pearl River is an utopian design of NL Architects from the Netherlands. It symbolically and practically links Hong Kong with Macau, Zhuhai and its Chinese hinterland to the west. The architects have designed a loop knot that transforms the left-hand traffic from Hong Kong to the right-hand traffic in Zhuhai and the rest of China. The bridge is suspended from floating islands that are covered with solar panels. Like nodes of a chain, artificial islands are strung along the bridge. According to the architects, "the transitions in the border area are designed to be fluent": it dances across the river delta in an organic and linear style. The bridge is intended to become the new symbol of a vibrant metropolis.

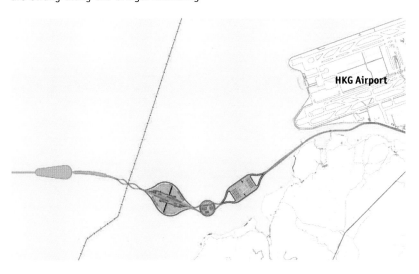

HKG Airport

Chek Lap Kok Airport
Cheong Hong Road, Chek Lap Kok
Norman Foster
1998

100 A

For the construction of the new airport in Hong Kong, Chek Lap Kok island, located 35 kilometres west of the city, was turned into a level area, 21 square kilometres in size: hills of up to 90 metres in height were removed and the size of the island increased four times using landfills in the sea. Politically the airport was a "parting gift" at the end of British colonial rule in 1997. Architectural bureau Foster and Partners of London had won the international design competition for the new hub, which replaced the old airport, Kai Tak. Their Y-shaped terminal is 1.27-kilometre-long making it the largest enclosed space ever built. The terminal offers 516,000 square

metres of space. A shuttle train runs back and forth inside the building. The terminal is made of lightweight metal shells, which were prefabricated in Singapore and the UK, each spanning 36 metres and creating a continuous barrel roof in an east-west direction. The light, bright hall facilitates orientation and offers views of the aprons. About five percent of the roof surfaces have clear glass panels. The terminal is located centrally between the two runways and has 39 passenger boarding bridges. The new airport is connected by bridges, tunnels and viaducts to the highway and railway network of Hong Kong. The traffic of departing and arriving passengers is kept separateon different floor levels. The terminal will be expanded in the future by a large X-shaped second terminal in the West.

4

A

100

099

✈ HKG

0   2.5   5.0
km

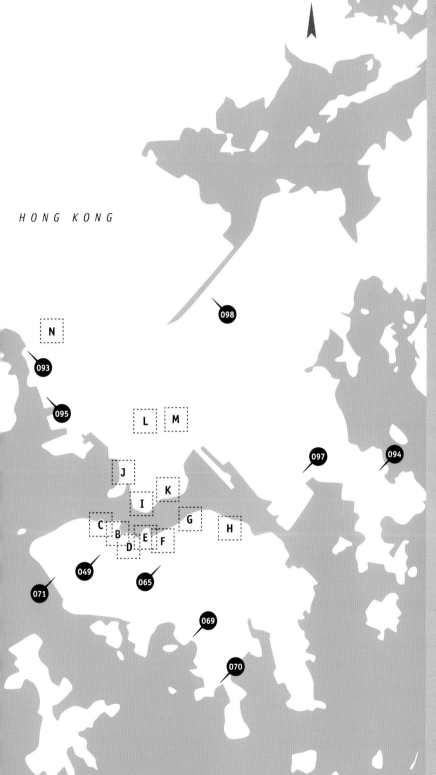

N

HONG KONG

098

N

093

095

L   M

097

094

J

K

I

C   G   H

B E F

D

049

065

071

069

070

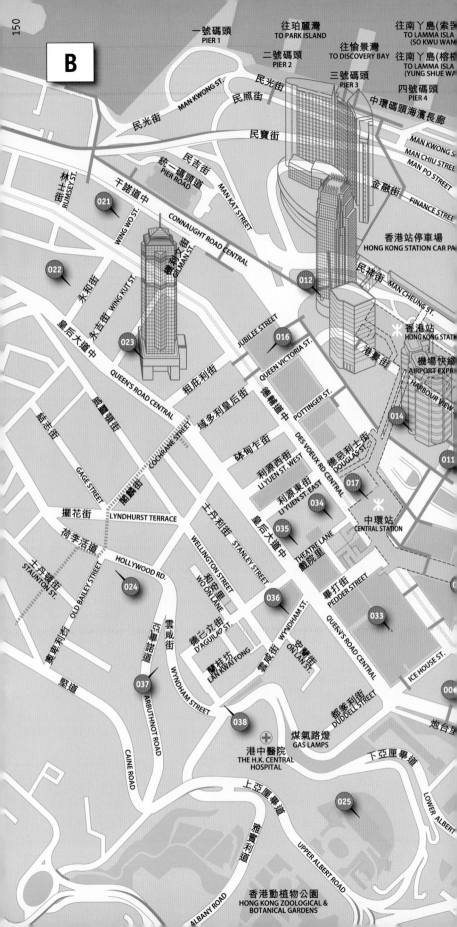

B

一號碼頭
PIER 1

往珀麗灣
TO PARK ISLAND

往南丫島(索罟
TO LAMMA ISLA
(SO KWU WAN

二號碼頭
PIER 2

往愉景灣
TO DISCOVERY BAY

往南丫島(榕樹
TO LAMMA ISLA
(YUNG SHUE WA

三號碼頭
PIER 3

四號碼頭
PIER 4

中環碼頭海濱長廊

民光街 MAN KWONG ST.

民光街

民照街

民寶街

MAN KWONG S
MAN CHIU STREE
MAN PO STREET

金融街
FINANCE STREE

民吉街

統一碼頭道
PIER ROAD

街士林 RUMSEY ST.

干諾道中

MAN KAT STREET

021

WING WO ST.

CONNAUGHT ROAD CENTRAL

香港站停車場
HONG KONG STATION CAR PA

022

永利街

永吉街 WING KUT ST.

GILMAN ST.

德輔道中

012

民祥街

MAN CHEUNG ST.

023

皇后大道中

QUEEN'S ROAD CENTRAL

租庇利街

JUBILEE STREET

016

德輔道中

港景街

香港站
HONG KONG STAT

德己立街

COCHRANE STREET

閣麟街

GAGE STREET

擺花街

LYNDHURST TERRACE

域多利皇后街

QUEEN VICTORIA ST.

砵甸乍街

POTTINGER ST.

利源西街
LI YUEN ST. WEST

利源東街
LI YUEN ST. EAST

DES VOEUX RD CENTRAL

德忌利士街

DOUGLAS ST.

機場快線
AIRPORT EXPR

HARBOUR VIEW

014

011

017

荷李活道

土丹頓街
STAUNTON ST.

土丹利街

STANLEY STREET

威靈頓街
WELLINGTON STREET

和安里
WO ON LANE

034

035

皇后大道中

QUEEN'S ROAD CENTRAL

戲院里

THEATRE LANE

中環站
CENTRAL STATION

024

HOLLYWOOD RD.

雲咸街

鴨巴甸街

OLD BAILEY STREET

德己立街
D'AGUILA ST.

蘭桂坊
LAN KWAI FONG

雲咸街 WYNDHAM ST.

安蘭街
ON LAN ST.

畢打街

PEDDER STREET

036

QUEEN'S ROAD CENTRAL

033

ICE HOUSE ST.

00

炮台里

037

ARBUTHNOT ROAD

堅道

WYNDHAM STREET

038

都爹利街

DUDDELL STREET

煤氣路燈
GAS LAMPS

下亞厘畢道

CAINE ROAD

港中醫院
THE H.K. CENTRAL
HOSPITAL

上亞厘畢道

LOWER ALBERT

025

雅賓利道

UPPER ALBERT ROAD

ALBANY ROAD

香港動植物公園
HONG KONG ZOOLOGICAL &
BOTANICAL GARDENS

N

往長洲
HEUNG CHAU
號碼頭
PIER 5
往坪洲
TO PENG CHAU
往大嶼山(梅窩)
TO LANTAU ISLAND (MUI WO)
六號碼頭
PIER 6
往尖沙咀
TO TSIM SHA TSUI
CENTRAL PIER WATERFRONT
七號碼頭
PIER 7
八號碼頭
PIER 8
中環碼頭
CENTRAL PIERS
九號碼頭
PIER 9
維多利亞港
VICTORIA HARBOUR

MAN YIU STREET

013

新中環海濱
NEW CENTRAL HARBOURFRONT

龍和道

D

039

廣場

CONNAUGHT PLACE

愛丁堡廣場
EDINBURGH PLACE

LUNG WO ROAD

愛丁堡廣場

040

干諾道中

010

015

添華道
TIM WA AVENUE

041

皇后像廣場
STATUE SQUARE

028

會所街
CLUB STREET

CONNAUGHT ROAD CENTRAL

和平紀念碑
CENOTAPH

001

美利道
MURRAY RD.

002

夏慤道

008

遮打道
CHATER ROAD

007

銀行街
BANK STREET

雪廠街
JACKSON RD.

遮打花園
CHATER GARDEN

琳寶徑
LAMBETH WALK

HARCOURT ROAD

029

042

德立街

添馬街

030

003

005

金鐘道

DRAKE STREET

終審法院
COURT OF FINAL
APPEAL

027

GARDEN ROAD

COTTON TREE DRIVE

TAMAR ST.

聖約翰座堂
ST. JOHN'S CATHEDRAL

031

004

茶具文物館
MUSEUM OF TEA WARE

32

花園道

紅棉路

QUEENSWAY

SUPREME

香港公園
HONG KONG PARK

柏運道
PARK AVENUE

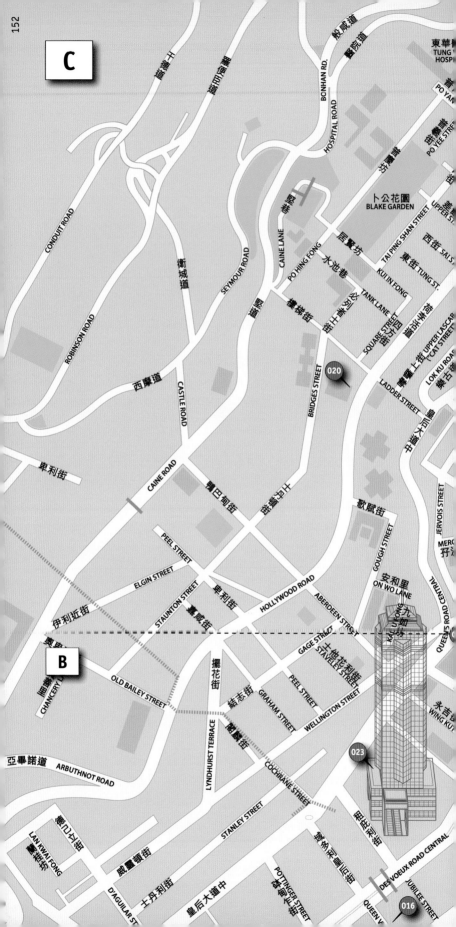

C

B

020

023

016

東華醫院
TUNG
HOSPITAL

PO YAN

PO YEE STREET

卜公花園
BLAKE GARDEN

堅城道 CONDUIT ROAD

羅便臣道 ROBINSON ROAD

西摩道 SEYMOUR ROAD

衞城道

西陵道

卑利街

堅道 CAINE ROAD

衛城道 CASTLE ROAD

伊利近街

奧卑利

忌連拿利

嘉咸街

士丹頓街 STAUNTON STREET

擺花街

卑利街

些利街

居賢坊

必列者士街

樓梯街

水池巷

PO HING FONG

CAINE LANE

TANK LANE

TAI PING SHAN STREET

西街 SAI S

東街 TUNG ST

KUI IN FONG

SQUARE STREET

UPPER ST

LADDER STREET

閣麟街

歌賦街

BRIDGES STREET

GOUGH STREET

PEEL STREET

ELGIN STREET

荷李活道 HOLLYWOOD ROAD

鴨巴甸街 ABERDEEN STREET

安和里
ON WO LANE

JERVOIS STREET

皇后大道中 QUEENS ROAD CENTRAL

MERC

孖沙

LOK KU ROAD

樂古道

摩羅上街 UPPER LASCAR

荷李活道 ("CAT STREET")

士他花利街
STAVELEY STREET

嘉威街 GAGE STREET

結志街

鴨巴甸街

卑利街 PEEL STREET

威靈頓街 WELLINGTON STREET

九如坊

KAU U FONG

亞畢諾道 ARBUTHNOT ROAD

OLD BAILEY STREET

LYNDHURST TERRACE

擺花街

鴨巴甸街

嘉咸街 GRAHAM STREET

忌連拿利

CHANCERY

闊蘭街

永吉街
WING KUT

租庇利街

蘭桂坊
LAN KWAI FONG

威靈頓街

德己立街 D'AGUILAR ST

士丹利街 STANLEY STREET

閣麟街 COCHRANE STREET

皇后大道中

擺列者士街

砵典乍街
POTTINGER STREET

機利文新街

機利文街

德輔道中 DES VOEUX ROAD CENTRAL

QUEEN V

JUBILEE STREET

中山紀念公園
SUN YAT SEN MEMORIAL PARK

N

新街
皇后大道西
QUEEN'S ROAD WEST
高陞街 KO SHING ST.
德輔道西
QUEEN STREET
皇后街
干諾道西
西消防街
德輔道西
DES VOEUX ROAD WEST

荷李活道公園
HOLLYWOOD ROAD PARK

WEST FIRE SERVICES STREET

POSSESSION ST.

中港道

文武廟
BONHAM STRAND WEST

CONNAUGHT ROAD WEST

中西區海濱長廊-上環段
CENTRAL AND WESTERN DISTRICT
PROMENADE - SHEUNG WAN SECTION

慶利臣街
文咸東街
新街市街
中景道
CHUNG KING ROAD

CHUNG KONG ROAD

019
NEW MARKET ST.
MORRISON STREET

WING LOK STREET
德輔道中

急庇利街

CLEVERLY ST.

018

港澳客輪碼頭
HK-MACAU FERRY TERMINAL

HILLIER ST.
上環站
SHEUNG WAN STATION

文華里

干諾道中

MAN WA LANE

021

林士街
RUMSEY ST.

WING WO ST.
CONNAUGHT ROAD CENTRAL
民吉街
民光街

MAN KWONG STREET

MAN KAT STREET
民寶街

利文街
STREET

D

堅尼地道

KENNEDY ROAD

聖佛蘭士街 ST. FRANCIS ST.

星街

月街 MOON ST.

皇后大道東

日街 SUN STREET

聯發街 LUN FAT STREET

機利臣街 GRESSON STREET

利節街 LI CHIT STREET

蘭杜街 LANDALE STREET

晏頓街 ANTON STREET

永豐街 WING FUNG STREET

STAR STREET

QUEEN'S ROAD EAST

莊士敦道 JOHNSTON ROAD

東美里 MONMOUTH PATH

正義道

軒尼詩道

HENNESSY ROAD

金鐘道

分域街

駱克道 LOCKHART ROAD

軍器廠街

052

金鐘停車場 ADMIRALTY CARPARK

謝斐道 FENWICK STREET

JAFFE ROAD

ARSENAL STREET

金鐘站 ADMIRALTY STATION

夏慤道

告士打道

GLOUCESTER ROAD

分域街

053

044

添美道

PERFORMING ARTS AVE. 演藝道

TIM ME AVENUE

分域碼頭街 FENWICK PIER STREET

龍滙道 LUNG WUI ROAD

龍景街 LUNG KING STREET

立法會道 LEGISLATIVE COUNCIL ROAD

添馬公園 TAMAR PARK

龍和道

維多利亞港
VICTORIA HARBOUR

N

波老道

BOWEN ROAD

賈雲道

BORRETT ROAD

波老道

麥當勞道

MAC DONNELL ROAD

堅尼地道

046

DRIVE

堅尼地道

047

048

法院道

026

KENNEDY ROAD

香港公園
HONG KONG PARK

045

SUPREME COURT ROAD

COTTON TREE DRIVE

B

031

添馬街

QUEENSWAY

紅棉路

004

花園道

GARDEN ROAD

005

003

043

030

TAMAR STREET

德立街 DRAKE ST.

042

美利道

遮打花園
CHATER GARDEN

041

002

晏臣道

添華道

HARCOURT ROAD

015

MURRAY ROAD

遮打道

CHATER ROAD

001

會所街
CLUB ST.

JACKSON RD.

028

TIM WA AVENUE

干諾道中

040

CONNAUGHT ROAD CENTRAL

愛丁堡廣場

愛丁堡廣場

LUNG WO ROAD

EDINBURGH PLACE

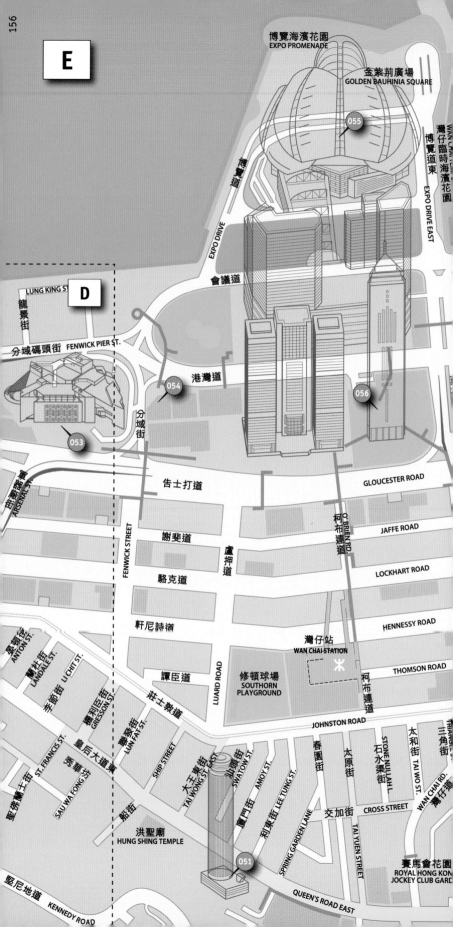

E

博覽海濱花園
EXPO PROMENADE

金紫荊廣場
GOLDEN BAUHINIA SQUARE

055

灣仔臨時海濱花園

博覽道

博覽道東
EXPO DRIVE EAST

博覽道
EXPO DRIVE

會議道

D

LUNG KING ST.
龍景街

分域碼頭街 FENWICK PIER ST.

港灣道

054

分域街

053

GLOUCESTER ROAD
告士打道

056

軍器廠街
ARSENAL ST.

FENWICK STREET
分域街

謝斐道

JAFFE ROAD

O'BRIEN RD.
柯布連道

LOCKHART ROAD

駱克道

盧押道

軒尼詩道

灣仔站
WAN CHAI STATION

HENNESSY ROAD

ANTON ST.
晏頓街

LANDALE ST.
蘭杜街

LI CHIT ST.
李節街

譚臣道

LUARD ROAD
盧押道

修頓球場
SOUTHORN
PLAYGROUND

THOMSON ROAD
柯布連道

GRESSON ST.
機利臣街

莊士敦道

LUN FAT ST.
聯發街

ST. FRANCIS ST.
聖佛蘭士街

SHIP STREET
船街

JOHNSTON ROAD

皇后大道東

TAI WONG ST. E.
大王東街

SWATOW ST.
汕頭街

AMOY ST.
廈門街

LEE TUNG ST.
利東街

SPRING GARDEN LANE
春園街

太原街

STONE NULLAH L.
石水渠街

TAI WO ST.
太和街

三角街

WAN CHAI RD.
灣仔道

SAU WA FONG
秀華坊

聖佛蘭士街

CROSS STREET
交加街

TAI YUEN STREET
太原街

賽馬會花園
ROYAL HONG KON
JOCKEY CLUB GARD

洪聖廟
HUNG SHING TEMPLE

051

KENNEDY ROAD
堅尼地道

QUEEN'S ROAD EAST

F

N

灣仔渡輪碼頭
WAN CHAI FERRY PIER

往紅磡及尖沙咀
HUNG HOM & TSIM SHA TSUI

鴻興道
HUNG HING ROAD

運盛街

WAN SHING STREET

馬師道

CONVENTION AVENUE

杜老誌道

灣仔運動場
WAN CHAI SPORTS GROUND

HARBOUR ROAD

057

MARSH ROAD

灣仔徑
HARBOUR DRIVE

告士打道

史釗域道

謝斐道

058

駱克道

TONNOCHY RD.

STEWART RD.

軒尼詩道

天樂里
TIN LOK LANE

WAN CHAI ROAD

050

臣道

莊士敦道

BURROWS ST.
巴路士街

MALLORY ST.
茂蘿街

柯布連道 HEARD ST.

灣仔道

CROSS LANE

活道

永祥街
WING CHEUNG ST.

交加里

TAK YAN ST.
德仁街

愛群道

日善街

崇賢里
SUNG YIN L.

摩理臣山道

YAT SIN STREET

崇德街
SUNG TAK ST.

MORRISON HILL ROAD

敦治醫院
ONJEE HOSPITAL

灣仔公園
WAN CHAI PARK

WOOD ROAD

敦誠里

SALVATION
ARMY ST.

OI KWAN ROAD

鄧肇堅醫院
TANG SHIU KIN
HOSPITAL

皇后大道東

WONG NAI CHUNG ROAD

STUBBS RD.

064

聿德里

HAU TAK LANE

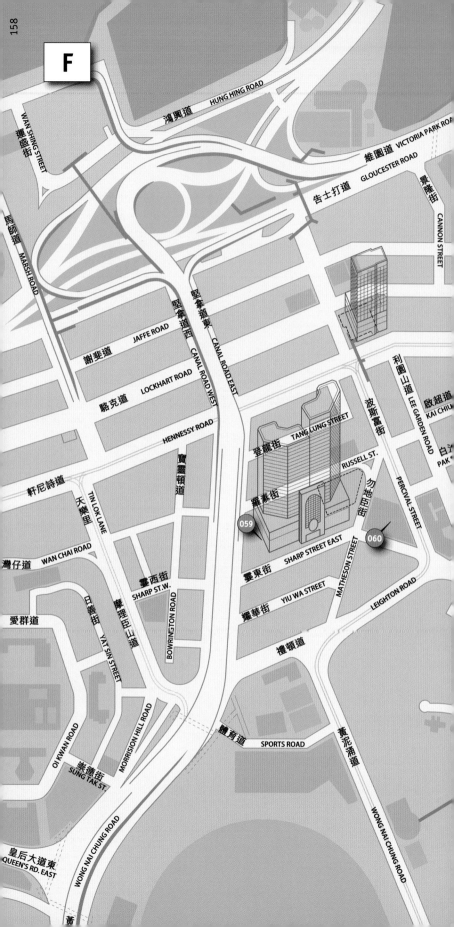

158

F

鴻興道 HUNG HING ROAD

運盛街 WAN SHING STREET

維園道 VICTORIA PARK ROAD

告士打道 GLOUCESTER ROAD

景隆街

CANNON STREET

馬師道 MARSH ROAD

謝斐道 JAFFE ROAD

堅拿道西

堅拿道東 CANAL ROAD EAST

CANAL ROAD WEST

駱克道 LOCKHART ROAD

軒尼詩道 HENNESSY ROAD

寶靈頓道

登龍街 TANG LUNG STREET

利園山道 LEE GARDEN ROAD

啟超道 KAI CHIU

白沙

PAK

波斯富街

羅素街 RUSSELL ST.

勿地臣街 PERCIVAL STREET

天樂里 TIN LOK LANE

灣仔道 WAN CHAI ROAD

059

060

雲西街 SHARP ST. W.

摩理臣山道

日善街 YAT SIN STREET

愛群道

BOWRINGTON ROAD

雲東街 SHARP STREET EAST

耀華街 YIU WA STREET

禮華街

MATHESON STREET

LEIGHTON ROAD

禮頓道

MORRISION HILL ROAD

OI KWAN ROAD

崇德街 SUNG TAK ST

體育道 SPORTS ROAD

黃泥涌道 WONG NAI CHUNG ROAD

皇后大道東 QUEEN'S RD. EAST

WONG NAI CHUNG ROAD

黃

N

加寧街 CLEVELAND ST.

厚誠街 HOUSTON ST.

百德新街 PATERSON ST.

京士頓街 KINGSTON ST.

告士打道 GLOUCESTER ROAD

告士頓街

記利佐治街 GREAT GEORGE STREET

銅鑼灣站
CAUSEWAY BAY STATION

怡和街 YEE WO STREET

糖街 SUGAR STREET

CAUSEWAY RD.

高士威道

摩頓台 MORETON TERR.

渣甸街 JARDINE'S BAZAAR

詞坊

邊寧頓街

伊榮街 IRVING STREET

JARDINE'S CRESCENT

FONG RD.

061

恩平道

LEIGHTON ROAD

銅鑼灣道

TUNG LO WAN RD.

希慎道 HYSAN AVENUE

新寧道

開平道

SUNNING ROAD

雲平道 YUN PING ROAD

PENNINGTON STREET

希雲街 HAVEN STREET

東院道

SUN WUI ROAD

不會道

062

開平道 HOI PING ROAD

禮頓道

棉花路 COTTON PATH

加路連山道 CAROLINE HILL ROAD

EASTERN HOSPITAL ROAD

禮頓山道

連道

加路連山道 CAROLINE HILL ROAD

LINK ROAD

TON HILL ROAD

BROADWOOD ROAD

樂活道

STADIUM PATH

063

N

東區走廊

糖水道

北角邨里
NORTH POINT EST. L.

WHARF ROAD

和富道

北角道

JAVA ROAD

TONG SHUI ROAD

CHUN YEUNG STREET

渣華道

春秧街

NORTH POINT ROAD

月圓街
YUET YUEN ST.

錦屏街

HEI WO ST.

英皇道

照利街

明園西街
MING YUEN WEST STREET

CHONG ST.

KING'S ROAD

北景街

KAM PING STREET

長康街

堡壘街

FORT STREET

孔雀道

CHEUNG HONG ST.

NORTH VIEW ST.

KIN WAH STREET

PEACOCK ROAD

建華街

清華街

CHING WAH STREET

TIN HAU TEMPLE RD. 天后廟道

炮台山道
FORTRESS HILL RD.

CLOUD VIEW RD.

雲景道

寶馬山道
BRAEMAR HILL ROAD

怡景道
ROAD

慧翠道
WAI TSUI CRESCENT

校園徑

HAU YUEN PATH

H

海瀾街 HOI CHAK STREET

芬尼街 FINNIE STREET

海堤街

海光街 'TS ONOMX IOH

海灣街

海壩街 HOI WAN STREET

東區海底隧道 Eastern Harbour Crossing

鰂魚涌公園·
QUARRY BAY PARK

HOI TAI STREET

糖廠街
TONG CHONG ST.

979

英皇道

太古坊
TAIKOO PLACE

華蘭路

20

068

濱海街

PAN HOI STREET

067

太古城道

WESTLANDS ROAD

7

船塢里

SHIPYARD LANE

1065

992

KING'S ROAD

1056

1094

43

鰂魚涌街

柏架山徑

祐民街

基利路

YAU MAN ST.

122

QUARRY BAY STREET

大潭郊野公園
（鰂魚涌擴建部分）
TAI TAM COUNTRY PARK
(QUARRY BAY EXTENSION)

衛奕信徑
WILSON TRAIL

GREIG ROAD

GREIG CRESCENT

基利坊

紅屋
WOOD SIDE

康愉街

HONG PAK PATH

康柏徑

HONG SHING ST

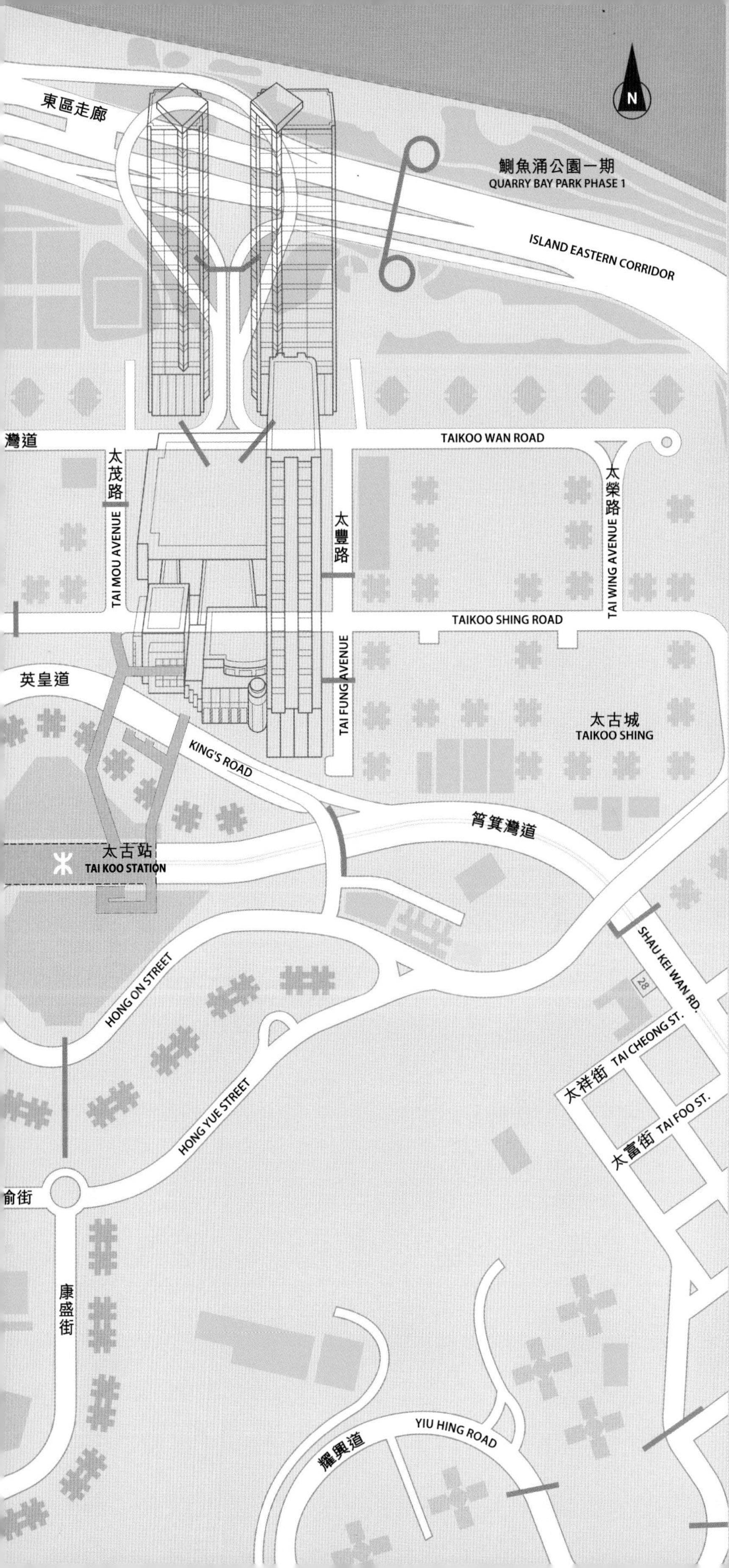

東區走廊

鰂魚涌公園一期
QUARRY BAY PARK PHASE 1

ISLAND EASTERN CORRIDOR

灣道

太茂路
TAI MOU AVENUE

太豐路

太古城
TAIKOO SHING

太榮路
TAI WING AVENUE

TAIKOO WAN ROAD

TAIKOO SHING ROAD

太豐道
TAI FUNG AVENUE

英皇道

KING'S ROAD

筲箕灣道

太古站
TAI KOO STATION

SHAU KEI WAN RD.

28

太祥街 TAI CHEONG ST.

太富街 TAI FOO ST.

HONG ON STREET

HONG YUE STREET

俞街

康盛街

YIU HING ROAD

耀興道

I

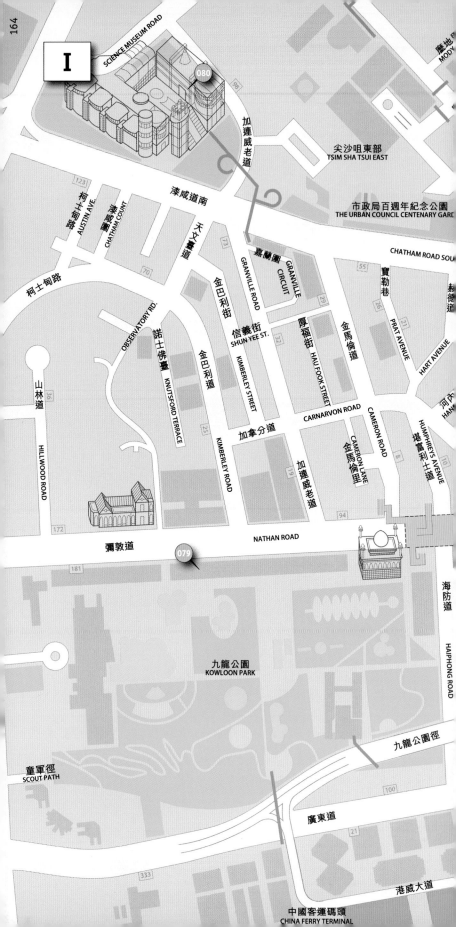

SCIENCE MUSEUM ROAD

080

加連威老道

尖沙咀東部
TSIM SHA TSUI EAST

市政局百週年紀念公園
THE URBAN COUNCIL CENTENARY GARD

123
安臣士柯
AUSTIN AVE.

漆咸海園
CHATHAM COURT

漆咸道南

天文臺道

73

嘉蘭圍
GRANVILLE CIRCUT

CHATHAM ROAD SOU

55
寶勒巷

赫德道

70

金巴利街

GRANVILLE ROAD

29

金馬倫道

PRAT AVENUE

HART AVENUE

柯士甸路

OBSERVATORY RD.

諾士佛臺
KNUTSFORD TERRACE

金巴利道

信義街
SHUN YEE ST.

32

KIMBERLEY STREET

厚福街
HAU FOOK STREET

26

河內
HAN

山林道

HILLWOOD ROAD

36

25

KIMBERLEY ROAD

加拿分道

CARNARVON ROAD

CAMERON ROAD

19

加連威老道

金馬倫里
CAMERON LANE

8

HUMPHREYS AVENUE

堪富利士道

172

94

彌敦道   NATHAN ROAD

079

海防道

181

九龍公園
KOWLOON PARK

九龍公園徑

童軍徑
SCOUT PATH

100

HAIPHONG ROAD

廣東道

21

333

中國客運碼頭
CHINA FERRY TERMINAL

港威大道

MODY

薩地

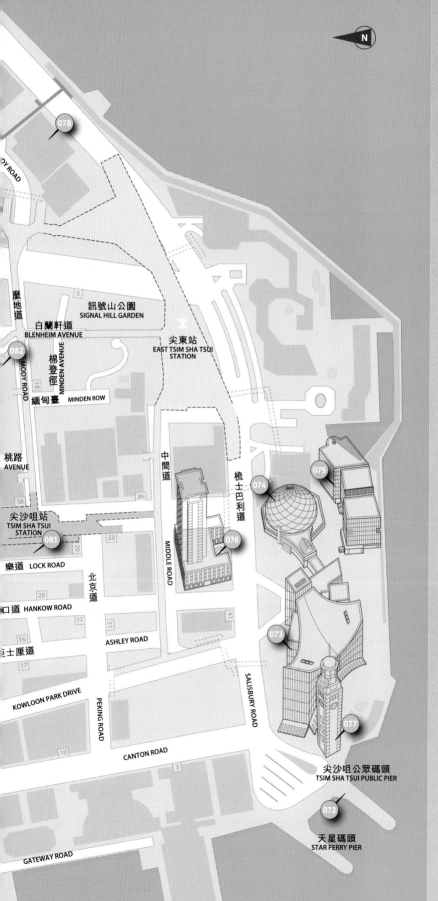

N

078

082

麼地道
MODY ROAD

白蘭軒道
BLENHEIM AVENUE

棉登徑

緬甸臺
MINDEN ROW

MINDEN AVENUE

訊號山公園
SIGNAL HILL GARDEN

尖東站
EAST TSIM SHA TSUI
STATION

桃路
AVENUE

尖沙咀站
TSIM SHA TSUI
STATION

081

樂道 LOCK ROAD

北京道

口道 HANKOW ROAD

士厘道

中間道

MIDDLE ROAD

梳士巴利道

074

076

075

073

ASHLEY ROAD

KOWLOON PARK DRIVE

PEKING ROAD

SALISBURY ROAD

CANTON ROAD

077

尖沙咀公眾碼頭
TSIM SHA TSUI PUBLIC PIER

072

天星碼頭
STAR FERRY PIER

GATEWAY ROAD

童軍徑
SCOUT PATH

柯士甸道
AUSTIN ROAD

柯士甸道西

廣東道
CANTON ROAD

匯民道
WUI MAN ROAD

柯士甸站
AUSTIN STATION

上海街

官涌街

廣東道

23

寶靈街

BOWRING STREET

393

KWUN CHUNG ST.
56

匯翔道
WUI CHEUNG ROAD

柯士甸站
AUSTIN STATION

臨時D1A(S)路
TEMPORARY ROAD D1A(S)

九龍佐治五世紀念公園
KING GEORGE V MEMORIAL
PARK, KOWLOON

46

佐敦道

39

廣東道

偉晴街

渡船街

JORDAN ROAD

臨時D1A(N)路

SHANGHAI STREET

南京街

炮台街

528

NANKING ST.

5

新填地街

文匯街

MAN WUI STREET

文成街

文英街

MAN YING STREET

寧波街
NING PO ST.

41

575

21

WAI CHING STREET

文苑街

MAN YUEN STREET

文蔚街

文昌街

MAN WAI STREET

MAN CHEONG STREET

MAN CHING STREET

TEMPORARY ROAD D1A(N)

48
RECLAMATION STREET

西貢街

50

SAIGON STREET

38

FERRY STREET

5.8

61

北海街
PAK HOI ST.

BATTERY STREET

甘肅街

KANSU STREET

欣翔道

YAN CHEUNG ROAD

CANTON ROAD

627

眾坊街

PUBLIC SQUARE STREET

澄平街

渡船街

YAU CHEUNG ROAD
友翔道

海泓道
HOI WANG ROAD

新填地街
RECLAMATION STREET

CHING PING STREET

FERRY STREET

KUN STREET

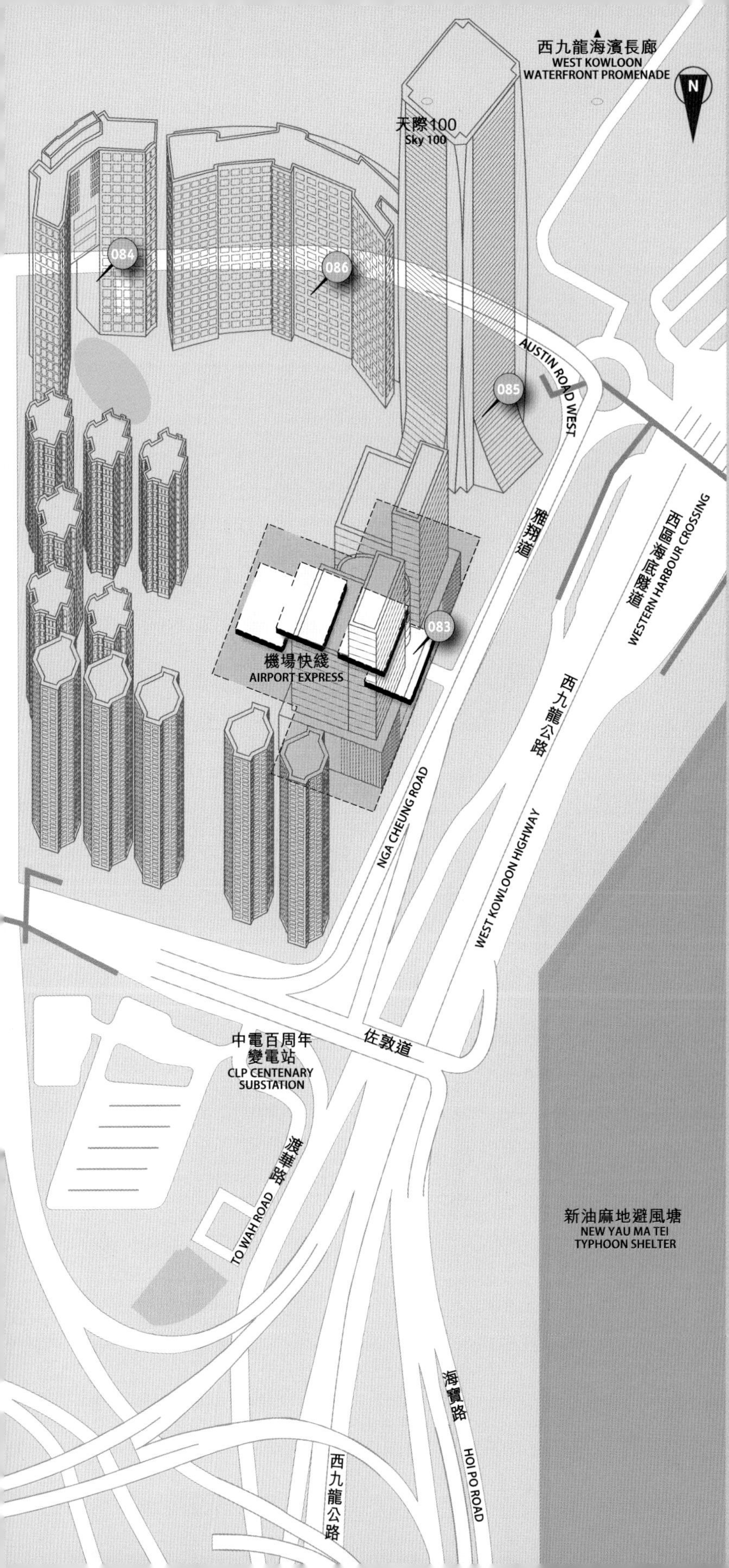

西九龍海濱長廊
WEST KOWLOON
WATERFRONT PROMENADE

N

天際100
Sky 100

084

086

085

AUSTIN ROAD WEST

雅翔道

WESTERN HARBOUR CROSSING
西區海底隧道

083

機場快綫
AIRPORT EXPRESS

NGA CHEUNG ROAD

西九龍公路
WEST KOWLOON HIGHWAY

佐敦道

中電百周年
變電站
CLP CENTENARY
SUBSTATION

TO WAH ROAD
海華路

新油麻地避風塘
NEW YAU MA TEI
TYPHOON SHELTER

海寶路
HOI PO ROAD

西九龍公路

K

尖沙咀東部
TSIM SHA TSUI EAST

087

加連威老道 GRANVILLE ROAD

科學館道 SCIENCE MUSEUM ROAD

漆咸道南 CHATHAM ROAD SOUTH

暢運道

麼地道

MODY ROAD

昌運道 CHEONG WAN ROAD

育才道

消防處九龍總部
FIRE SERVICES DEPARTMENT
KOWLOON HEADQUARTERS

海底隧道收費廣場
CROSS HARBOUR
TUNNEL TOLL PLAZA

康莊道
HONG CHONG RO

海底隧道
CROSS HARBOUR TUNNEL

梳士巴利道   SALISBURY ROAD

安運道 ON WAN ROAD

西鐵線
WEST RAIL LINE

紅磡站
HUNG HOM STATION

088

089

暢運道

巴士總站
BUS TERMINUS

昌運道 CHEONG WAN ROAD

都會道   METROPOLIS DRIVE

暢運道南   CHEONG WAN ROAD SOUTH

紅荔道

紅磡繞道

紅樂道   HUNG LOK ROAD

紅荔道

建灣街 KIN WAN STREET

紅磡道

HUNG HOM BYPASS

愛景街 OI KING STREET

紅鸞道
HUNG LUEN ROAD

德豐街 TAK FUNG STREET

N

090

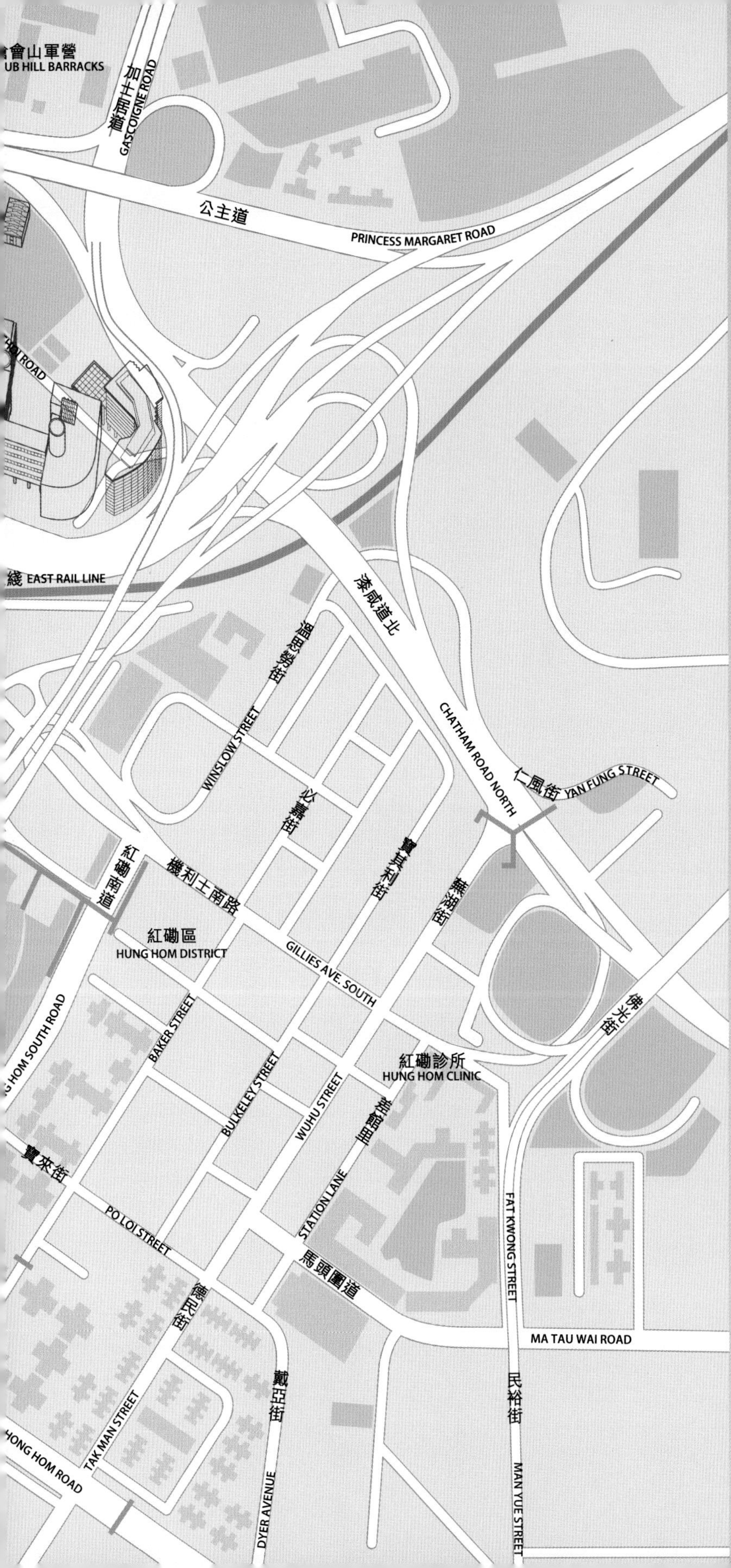

會山軍營
UB HILL BARRACKS

加士居道
GASCOIGNE ROAD

公主道
PRINCESS MARGARET ROAD

ROAD

綫 EAST RAIL LINE

漆咸道北
CHATHAM ROAD NORTH

仁風街 YAN FUNG STREET

屋梨活街
WINSLOW STREET

必嘉街

寶其利街

蕪湖街

紅磡南道
HUNG HOM SOUTH ROAD

機利士南路

紅磡區
HUNG HOM DISTRICT

紅磡道

GILLIES AVE. SOUTH

紅磡診所
HUNG HOM CLINIC

佛光街

BAKER STREET

寶英街
PO LOI STREET

BULKELEY STREET

WUHU STREET

差館里

STATION LANE

馬頭圍道

FAT KWONG STREET

馬頭圍道
MA TAU WAI ROAD

民裕街

庇利街

黃埔街

HONG HOM ROAD

TAK MAN STREET

戴亞街
DYER AVENUE

MAN YUE STREET

170

L

棠蔭街 TONG YAM STREET

大坑東道

TAI HANG TUNG ROAD

TAI HANG TUNG ROAD

龍珠街 LUNG CHU ST.

MAGNOLIA ROAD

丹桂路

石竹路 DIANTHUS ROAD

高瑰路 CASSIA ROAD

玫瑰街 ROSE STREET

牡丹路 PEONY ROAD

紫藤路 WISTARIA ROAD

海棠路

瑰麗路

桃源L

地錦路 VERBENA ROAD

又一居道

桃源街遊樂場 TO YUEN STREET PLAYGROUND

達之路

BEGONIA ROAD

GRANDEUR ROAD

PARC OASIS ROAD

花園街

雀僑街 TSEUK KIU ST.

TAT CHEE AVENUE

舒梨道 SURREY LANE

FA PO STREET

多福

金巴倫道 CUMBERLAND ROAD

律倫街

約道

雅息士道

施他佛道 STAFFORD ROAD

RUTLAND QUAD

YORK ROAD

ESSEX CRESCENT

窩打老道

打比道 DERBY RD.

對衡道

劍橋道

CAMBRIDGE ROAD

蘭開夏道 LANCASHIRE ROAD

慕禮道 MORAY RD.

西谷道 SELKIRK RD.

衡州道 HAMPSHIRE RD.

渭州道 WILTSHIRE RD.

禧福道 HEREFORD ROAD

DURHAM ROAD

牛津道 OXFORD ROAD

LA SALLE ROAD

喇沙利道

092

香港城市大學
CITY UNIVERSITY OF HK

達之路

歌和老街
CORNWALL STREET

歌和老街公園
CORNWALL STREET PARK

根德道公園
KENT ROAD GARDEN

真光里
TRUE LIGHT L.

KENT ROAD

根德道

YUEN STREET

O FUK ROAD

九龍塘站
KOWLOON TONG STATION

森麻實道

德雲道

DEVON ROAD

共運輸交滙處
BLIC TRANSPORT
INTERCHANGE

福道

沙福道

DORSET CRESCENT

歌和老街兒童遊樂場
CORNWALL STREET
CHILDREN'S PLAYGROUND

TIM FUK ROAD

SUFFOLK ROAD

SOMERSET ROAD

多實街

WATERLOO ROAD

窩打老道

聯合道

香港浸信會醫院
HONG KONG
BAPTIST HOSPITAL

香港浸會大學善衡校園
HONG KONG BAPTIST UNIVERSITY
HO SIN HANG CAMPUS

JUNCTION ROAD

N

聯福道

RENFREW ROAD

M

東隆道

九龍寨城公園
KOWLOON WALLED CITY PARK

培民街
PUI MAN STREET

東頭邨
TUNG TAU ESTATE

TUNG LUNG ROAD

東頭村道

靜安街
TSING ON STREET

東發道
TUNG FAT RD.

HENG LAM STREET

樂富遊樂場
LOK FU RECREATION GROUND

摩士公園(四號公園)
MORSE PARK (PARK NO.4)

杏林街

東泰里 TUNG TAI LANE

鳳舞街

TUNG TAU TSUEN ROAD

摩士公園(三號公園)
MORSE PARK (PARK NO.3)

橫頭磡

橫頭磡

橫頭磡東道

正德街

FUNG MO STREET

富美街

CHING TAK STREET

WANG TAU HOM EAST

摩士公園游泳池
MORSE PARK SWIMMING POOL

龍翔道

延文禮士道 INVERNESS ROAD

N

浸會大學道 BAPTIST UNIVERSITY ROAD

九龍仔遊樂場
KOWLOON TSAI PARK

富安街

樂富公園
LOK FU PARK

091

樂富站
LOK FU STATION

富仲道

FU ON STREET

聯合道公園
JUNCTION ROAD PARK

WANG TAU HOM SOUTH RD.

JUNCTION ROAD

富強街

WANG TAU HOM CENTRAL RD.

橫頭磡邨
NG TAU HOM ESTATE

FU KUENG STREET

竹園道

廣播道

FU MEI STREET

富裕街

FU YUE

馬可尼道
MARCONI RD.

BROADCAST DRIVE

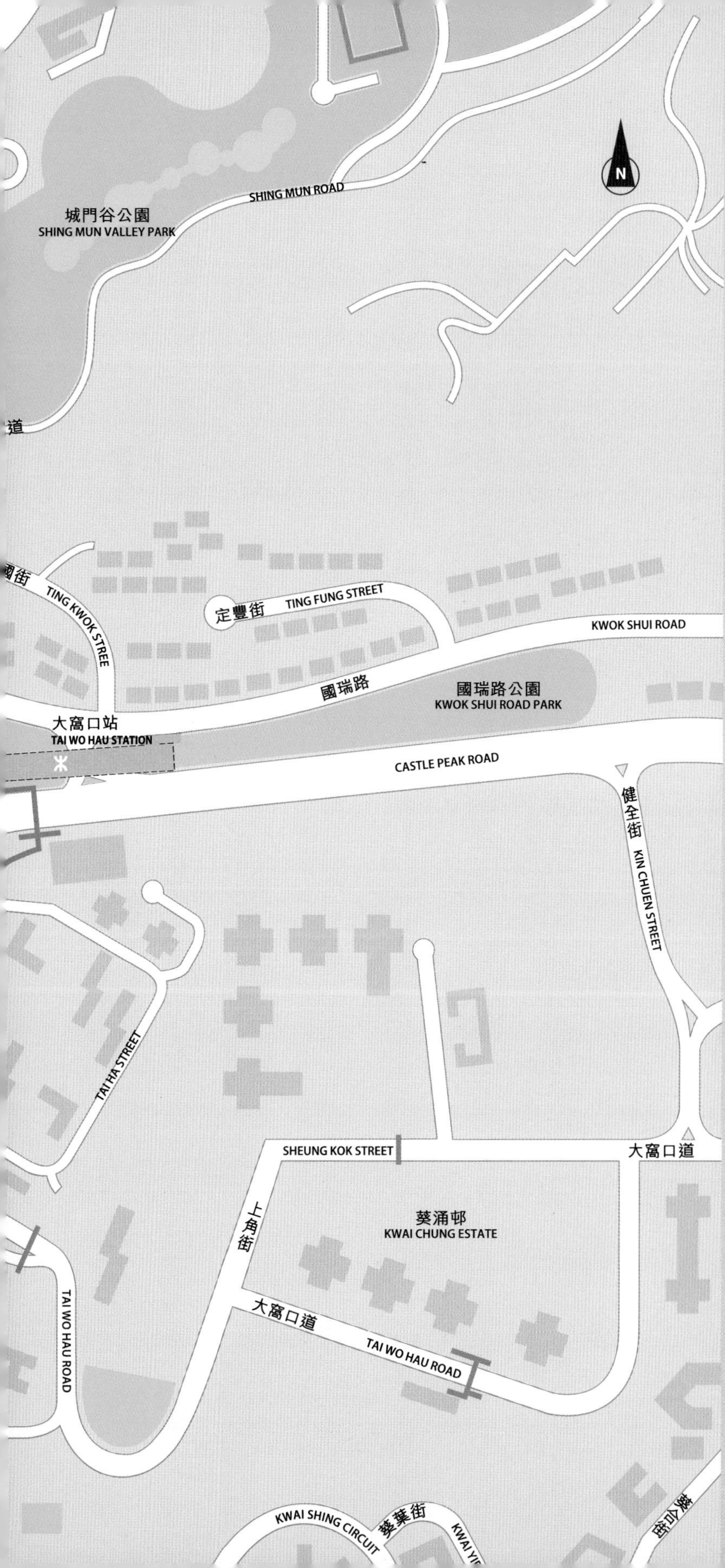

城門谷公園
SHING MUN VALLEY PARK

SHING MUN ROAD

道

閣街

TING KWOK STREE

定豐街 TING FUNG STREET

KWOK SHUI ROAD

國瑞路

國瑞路公園
KWOK SHUI ROAD PARK

大窩口站
TAI WO HAU STATION

CASTLE PEAK ROAD

健全街

KIN CHUEN STREET

TAI HA STREET

SHEUNG KOK STREET

大窩口道

上角街

葵涌邨
KWAI CHUNG ESTATE

大窩口道

TAI WO HAU ROAD

TAI WO HAU ROAD

KWAI SHING CIRCUIT

葵葉街

KWAI YI

City Development in Hong Kong

Competing with the internationally acclaimed city of Shanghai and the nearby Pearl River Delta, Hong Kong seemed on the verge of losing its economic and political significance when it was returned to China in 1997. However, the metropolis with its seven million inhabitants soon returned to rank among the global cities thanks to major city development projects. Today, Hong Kong is a special administrative district of China, and forms the southernmost part of a region which goes beyond the special economic district of Shenzhen and the industrial zone in Dongguan, reaching through to Guangzhou. The Pearl River Delta has long since become the world's biggest industrial factory, and is thus one of the drivers in the Chinese economic miracle.

When department manager Edward Li stares out of his window, he looks out onto the Silhouette of Kowloon, the peninsula in front of the dense jungle of buildings on Hong Kong Island. The sky is cloudy today, with fog and rain. In spite of this, the urban planner still enthuses about the big ideas for Victoria Harbour on the other side of the bay. Within the space of just one generation, a new district is to be created, with parks and leisure space where pilots once landed with their jumbo jets with a special license for Kai Tak Airport. The old airport building has long since been demolished, and the new terminal for cruise ships soars above the southern end of the take off and landing strip. The shape of the city will forever show the artificial strip of land, which caused not only the pilots to break into a sweat with their landing manoeuvres. Kai Tak connected Hong Kong to the rest of the world for decades, and now you cannot expect the old airport to simply disappear from the face of the city and

people's memories in the blink of an eye. You can hear a hint of nostalgia in the urban planner's words.

The user-friendly Chek Lap Kok Airport, which has received numerous prizes over the years, and which the British architect Norman Foster handed over to the Chinese authorities in 1998, was the last major project by the colonial rulers on an artificial island 30 kilometres west of the business centre — and this distance was reduced to a short trip with the new airport railway — a trip that is much faster than the time that used to take to travel between Kai Tak and Hong Kong Island. Building the new airport gave Hong Kong, a city characterised by an almost insatiable hunger for land, almost 250 hectares of inner-city building space practically overnight. However, right after the city airport was closed the airstrips were examined under the supervision of toxicologists, who ascertained the presence of kerosene and oil in the ground, as well as toxic heavy metals. Since then, one fifth of the site has been decontaminated, underground fuel tanks have been removed and almost all of the buildings have been demolished.

Today, all that can be seen of the former Kai Tak Airport is the small strip, which stretches into the sea like a breakwater. When the airport was being built, the hydraulics engineers used the construction rubble from the airport to reinforce the sea floor, to save costs and make logistics easier — despite contamination from the concrete. A spray was used to seal the fragments from the strip, which were then sunk forever in the sea.

The urban planning patterns for the new district, which is simply called South East Kowloon Development in the plans, hardly differ from the monotonous swathes

View of land reclamation in Central towards Two IFC

Housing and Property

Source: Government of the Hong Kong Special Administrative Region

Permanent living quarters by type

Type	2007 Number	%	2011 Number	%	2012 Number	%
Public rental housing units[1]	713,000	28.5	748,000	28.7	766,000	29.1
Subsidised sale flats[1][2]	398,000	15.9	391,000	15.0	391,000	14.8
Private permanent quarters[2][3]	1,392,000	55.6	1,465,000	56.3	1,480,000	56.1
Total	2,503,000 (+0.6)	100.0	2,603,000 (+0.5)	100.0	2,637,000 (+1.3)	100.0

Figures are as at the end of September of the year
[1] *Public rental housing units sold by the Housing Authority are classified as subsidised sale flats.*
[2] *Subsidised sale flats include quarters sold by the Housing Authority and Hong Kong Housing Society that cannot be traded in the open market. Those flats that can be traded in the open market are classified as private permanent quarters.*
[3] *Figures include all quarters used for residential purpose as well as those non-residential quarters usually with people living therein. Quarters known to be used for non-residential purpose and those in hotels and institutions are excluded.*

Property transactions

Value of registered Agreements for Sale and Purchase of property (HK$ billion)

	2007	2011	2012
Residential property	434.0	442.5	452.3
Non-residential property	91.6	145.4	201.7
Total	525.6 (+66.8)	587.6 (-14.7)	654.0 (+11.2)

Property price index[4] (Year 1999 = 100)

	2007	2011	2012
Private domestic units	103.5 (+11.7)	182.1 (+20.7)	206.0[#] (+13.1)[#]
Private offices (Grades A, B and C)	165.5 (+18.8)	297.9 (+29.3)	333.7[#] (+12.0)[#]

Property rental index[4] (Year 1999 = 100)

	2007	2011	2012
Private domestic units	101.8 (+11.1)	134.0 (+11.9)	142.6[#] (+6.4)[#]
Private offices (Grades A, B and C)	131.9 (+12.4)	169.9 (+15.1)	188.1[#] (+10.7)[#]

[4] *Figures are annual indices*
[#] *Provisional figures*

Newly completed residential flats by type

Type	2007 Number	2007 %	2011 Number	2011 %	2012 Number	2012 %
Public rental housing units	4,800	27.8	17,800	65.3	9,800	49.1
Subsidised sale flats	2,000	11.6	0	0	0	0
Private flats	10,500	60.6	9,400	34.7	10,100	50.9
Total	17,300 (-17.8)	100.0	27,200 (+30.3)	100.0	19,900 (-26.8)	100.0

Newly completed private buildings by end-use

End-use	2007	2011	2012
Total usable floor area [5]	**1,030,000** (-25.8)	**991,000** (-13.0)	**1,394,000** (+40.7)
Residential	451,000 (-36.9)	472,000 (-22.9)	558,000 (+18.2)
Commercial	333,000 (+56.2)	216,000 (+24.5)	226,000 (+5.0)
Industrial	15,000 (-47.3)	129,000 (+265.8)	197,000 (+52.4)
Others	230,000 (-46.7)	175,000 (-45.2)	414,000 (+136.8)
Total Cost of construction (HK$ billion)	**21.8**	**24.5**	**51.3**

Private buildings with consent to commence work by end-use

End-use	2007	2011	2012
Total usable floor area [5][6]	**991,000** (+34.4)	**719,000** (-17.5)	**1,278,000** (+77.8)
Residential	588,000 (+57.9)	335,000 (+40.1)	630,000 (+88.5)
Commercial	185,000 (-0.8)	91,000 (-38.8)	209,000 (+130.4)
Industrial	91,000 (+746.2)	109,000 (+218.6)	46,000 (-57.7)
Others	126,000 (-24.5)	184,000 (-59.1)	392,000 (+112.8)

[5] Usable floor area of '000 sqm
[6] Figures refer to usable floor areas of building projects for which the plans are submitted to the building authority for approval for the first time.

Figures in brackets refer to percentage changes over the same period in the prior year and are calculated based on unrounded figures.

In City Gallery (3 Edinburgh Place, Central), the urban planners of HK government present new projects from Wednesday to Monday (10am to 6pm).

of skyscrapers which stretch along the coast. The various buildings are also constructed in a very similar manner: the towers are either set on cross-shaped foundations in order to offer the greatest possible surface for windows, or they are of staggered height to afford a large number of apartments with views over the bay. The new district has almost ten times more inhabitants than the average in Hong Kong, with 53,000 people per square kilometre. Even the presence of the parks, which appear among the jungle of houses like aisles, can hardly alter this ratio.

This gigantic residential construction project in European terms is part of a series of city development initiatives which have made Hong Kong attractive again for foreign real estate agents. Whereas in East Kowloon one third of the apartments being built are public rental housing units, in the past few years a kind of counter-model has been realised. This district, in the picturesque Discovery Bay, does not have any disruptive cars; however it does have a yacht harbour and direct ferry connections to Hong Kong Island. Broad sea-front promenades and an even wider sandy beach give a feeling of always being on vacation. It seems as if the leisure business has made itself at home here. If it were not for the 20-storey blocks apartment buildings, the make-believe fishing village could certainly be seen as making a contribution to the new urbanism movement.

On the small strip of coast on Hong Kong Island, which is well known from the postcard view from the Peak, a lot has changed since the British troops left in 1997. Dominant new buildings have made a major impact on the face of the city. This starts with the conference and exhibition

Density: people/km²

4,583
5,163
5,570
6,032
6,168
6,413

7.0 million
7.08
6.81
6.66
6.15
5.70
6.0 million
5.06
5.0 million
0
4.0 million
1.0 million
3.0 million
2.0 million

Between 1985 and 2010 the number of HK inhabitants increased by 30%.

Source: Stefan Al: Factory Towns of South China. An illustrated guidebook. Hong Kong 2012

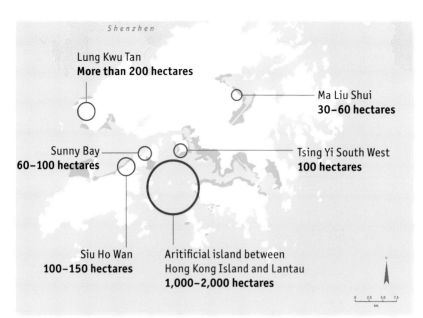

Land reclamation in Hong Kong since 1850 and potential reclamation area until 2030
(Source: Hong Kong Development Bureau/South China Morning Post)

centre, which was designed by Chicago-based architectural practice of Skidmore, Owings & Merrill in the form of a lotus blossom, and also includes the new offices for Hong Kong's Chief Executive, with the parliament and ministers' offices, as well as the IFC One and Two complexes designed by César Pelli. These three major projects have been erected on land that has been regained since the early 1990s. A strip of up to 500 metres in breadth has been built up in front of the historic silhouette of Central, Admiralty and Wan Chai, which is to be further developed in the coming years. From here, it will be possible to look to the new districts to the east around the former Kai Tak Airport. However, the view will also include West Kowloon, the third major project in central Hong Kong, which has attracted attention thanks to land reclamation and flagship buildings such as the ICC Tower by Kohn Pedersen Fox.

A new product on the real estate market has also been setting architectural standards, in terms of building types, since the end of the 1990s: apartments which only differ from hotels in that you bring your own furniture. This product can now also be found in European real estate portfolios. This type of project has also been erected in Happy Valley, where Hong Kong's only horse racing track attracts thousands of gambling visitors every week. At the foot of Leighton Hill, eight 30-storey building shells soar up into the sky. The floor plans are based on the principles of Feng Shui with the towers arranged in waves, while the bases house parking garages, service rooms and even a ballroom. Private needs such as sunbathing, swimming lessons and fitness training are all catered for the upper storeys which afford superb views over the skyline. In the "sleeping floors", catering and cleaning services ensure that the residents are well cared for around the clock: they just have to show their Leighton Hill club card to use the services.

These projects can hardly be surpassed in terms of exclusivity and are prime examples of the fact that the fear of an economic dictatorship once held when Hong Kong was taken back over by communist China seems to have totally dissolved. It is much rather the case that Happy Valley, or residential districts favoured by the top dogs in the economy such as Tai Tam, Peak, Sai Kung, Clearwater Bay, Pok Fu Lam, Mid Levels, Repulse Bay, Stanley or Discovery Bay, show that the real estate market in Hong Kong offers the most exclusive and most expensive locations in the whole of Asia.

Jonathan Andrews

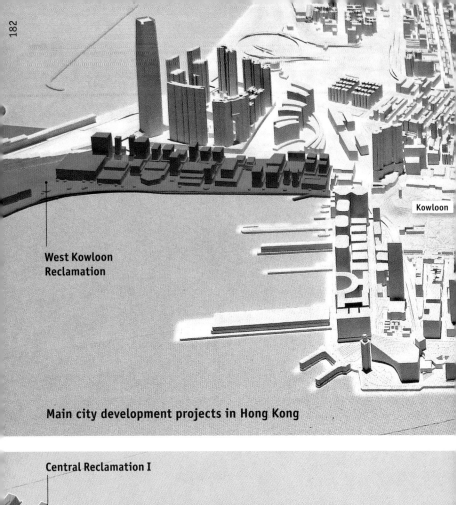

West Kowloon
Reclamation

Kowloon

Main city development projects in Hong Kong

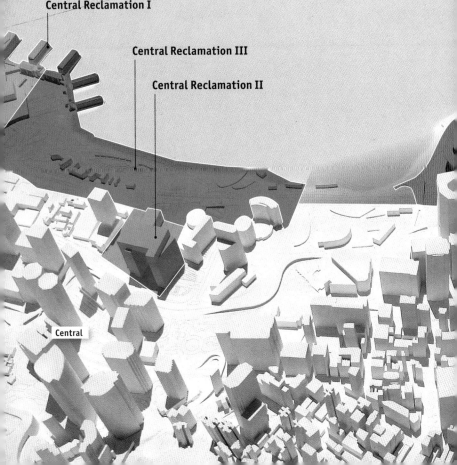

Central Reclamation I

Central Reclamation III

Central Reclamation II

Central

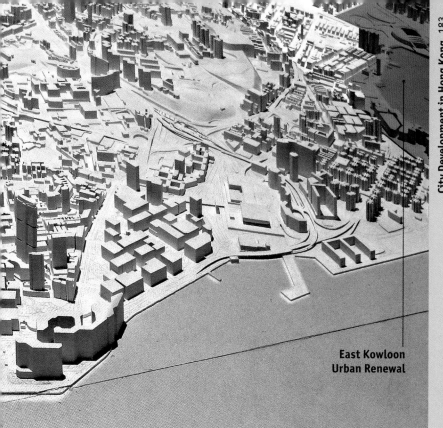

East Kowloon
Urban Renewal

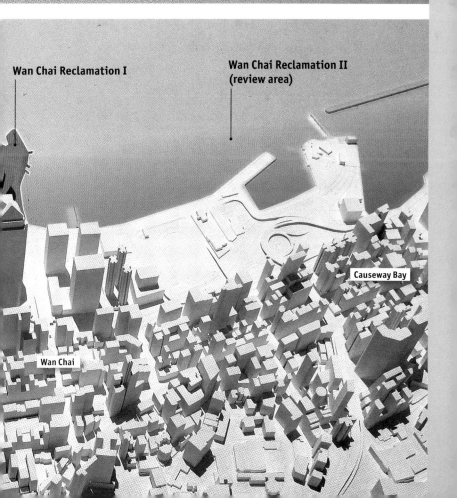

Wan Chai Reclamation I

Wan Chai Reclamation II
(review area)

Causeway Bay

Wan Chai

New land in Central and Wan Chai

The most elaborate land reclamation after the new airport is currently being realized on Hong Kong's north coast. In the Wan Chai and Central districts, characterized by their office blocks, new areas in five sub-sections of up to 500 metres are being built in Victoria Harbour. This major project was discussed for the first time in the middle of the 1980s. The first phase in Wan Chai was completed in 1997 with the construction of the Hong Kong Convention and Exhibition Centre (HKCEC). At present, the largest project is underway with the third phase in Central. Here, a tunnel, the Central-Wan Chai Bypass, is to run under the new business district. Completion is scheduled for 2017. Then office towers and a park will be built here.

Cultural district in West Kowloon

A new district is being created right now in West Kowloon, and this is to be developed to become a cultural centre by 2017. To the south of the residential and office buildings around Union Square, famous architects such as Norman Foster, Rocco Yim and Rem Koolhaas have designed museums, theatres and cultural hubs. In 2011 Foster's concept was selected for further development. A project costs of almost three billion euros has now been forecast for the new district. A city park is to be created at the western tip.

Union Square

West Kowloon

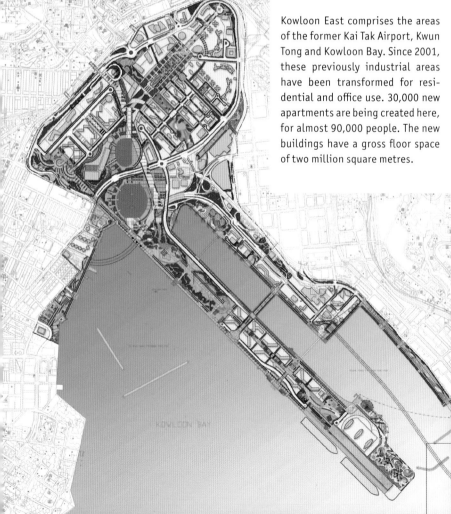

Residential areas in Kowloon East

Kowloon East comprises the areas of the former Kai Tak Airport, Kwun Tong and Kowloon Bay. Since 2001, these previously industrial areas have been transformed for residential and office use. 30,000 new apartments are being created here, for almost 90,000 people. The new buildings have a gross floor space of two million square metres.

Kowloon Bay

Kwun Tong

Buildings
Digits indicate the project number

Architects
Digits indicate the project numbers

Author

Ulf Meyer, born in 1970, studied at
the Berlin Technical University and the
Illinois Institute of Technology in
Chicago. Between 2008 and 2010 he was
Assistant Professor for sustainable
urban design at Kansas State University
in Manhattan/Kansas and in 2010–2011
was Hyde Chair of Excellence at the UNL
(University of Nebraska-Lincoln). An acclaimed author and editor of several pub-
lications on contemporary architecture,
he lectures at universities and cultural
centres in Europe, USA and Canada as well
as Japan, China, Singapore, Australia,
Malaysia, the Philippines and Taiwan.

The *Deutsche Nationalbibliothek* lists this publication in the *Deutsche National-bibliografie*; detailed bibliographic data are available on the Internet at *http://dnb.d-nb.de.*

ISBN 978-3-86922-201-1

DOM
publishers

© 2013 by DOM publishers, Berlin
www.dom-publishers.com

Translation
Ulf Meyer

Final editing
Uta Keil

Photo editing
Tanja Reith

Final proofreading
Mariangela Palazzi-Williams

Design
Masako Tomokiyo

QR-Codes
Christoph Gößmann

Maps
MTR Corporation, Hong Kong

Printing
Tiger Printing (Hong Kong) Co., Ltd.
www.tigerprinting.hk